"I love Joey's passion for disciple-making and adventure. When we follow Jesus closely and stay in close proximity to others, we fulfill Jesus' Great Commission and the kingdom is impacted. I recommend reading *DiscipleTrip* to anyone who is serious about being a disciple of Jesus!"

-Mark Batterson
New York Times best-selling author of *The Circle Maker*
Lead Pastor of National Community Church

"Following Christ was never intended to be boring nor a solo endeavor! Jesus gives us a clear plan to make maximum impact by making disciples and Joey's book clearly explains that process. His stories of adventure will make you laugh, and his vulnerability is refreshing. I HIGHLY recommend reading *DiscipleTrip* to anyone who is passionate about following Christ!"

-Brian Bloye
Co-Author of *It's Personal*
Senior Pastor of West Ridge Church

DiscipleTrip

Live the Adventure

By Dr. Joey Cook

With Joanna Sanders

Cover Design: Daniel Tyler, Joe Snyder, & Propel Marketing, LLC
Cover Photo: Joe Poulson
Editing: Joanna Sanders & Propel Marketing, LLC
Layout & Formatting: Joanna Sanders & Propel Marketing, LLC
Author's Photo Credit: Propel Marketing, LLC

Dedicated to Ryder & MJ:

I have written this book so that you can know how Jesus has designed us to live.

You are my inspiration, and you will always be my beloved son and daughter; no matter how many mountains you climb, or how many times you fall.

Here's to many more adventures with you both…

-Dad

Contents

Preface: Warning & Advisory

THE PURPOSE OF THIS BOOK is to challenge you to grow dynamically with Christ. You will be learning some things. You will be unlearning others, for the purpose of sanctification. The trip includes a shift in perspective from the surface of the temporal to the deep of the spiritual; the eternal. This journey is not about sitting in a pew, or listening to a sermon, only to be dismissed quietly and leave unchanged. Are you ready for true adventure?

The first DiscipleTrip, ever, commenced with Jesus' very words in Matthew 4:19, "Follow Me," and it changed everyone on the trip.

What do we mean by the term "DiscipleTrip?" A DiscipleTrip is the unstructured, undefined, adventure-filled walk that occurs when Jesus is at the center of life and relationships. It is our term for conveying what discipleship was really intended to look like; as mirrored by Jesus and removed from man's strategy, merchandising, structure, or the idea that we must go far away to be "on mission." A DiscipleTrip is what we are all called to as followers of Jesus. A DiscipleTrip *is* the mission trip that started the moment we said "yes" to Christ being our Lord and Savior.

It is when we begin this relationship that we can begin to live and walk according to His calling for our lives. His final proclamation in the Gospel according to Matthew is found in chapter 28, verses 19 and 20. It is His personal call to us all, to embark on a DiscipleTrip:

"GO THEREFORE AND MAKE DISCIPLES OF ALL NATIONS, BAPTIZING THEM IN THE NAME OF THE FATHER AND OF THE SON AND OF THE HOLY

Spirit, teaching them to observe all that I have commanded you. And behold, I am with you always, to the end of the age."

This is Jesus' command to His followers to engage in the process of disciple-making and it is this premise that serves as the inspiration for the concept of *DiscipleTrip*. A DiscipleTrip entails the adventure of following Jesus in the company of others, thus resulting in creating other disciples, or students, of Jesus; never of our own.

And that is where the warning takes root. Engaging in the ancient practice of disciple-making does not grant us favor with God and does not in itself make us wise or good. The Bible tells us that the fear of the Lord is the beginning of wisdom (Prov 9:10) and that none are righteous or good (Romans 3:10). Making disciples should be more reflective of obedient hearts proceeding in acts of worship, rather than strategies for "ministry." Loving God and loving people *is not* the Gospel; but the summation of all of the law and the prophets. Following the law cannot earn our righteousness. We can do our best works and they will not be enough. The ones who truly benefit from the process of disciple-making are those that begin from, and proceed in, humble and teachable spirits. It is only in finding ourselves as recipients of God's grace that we can begin to engage in helping others find it, as well.

We must fix our eyes on His finished work on the cross, in order to properly adventure with Him by the power of the Holy Spirit. You'll read many stories here of our own adventures that have taken us to many "unexpected" places. Although no actual road trip is required in a DiscipleTrip, we can be assured that our DiscipleTrip will have us hitting the road with Jesus, never to return the same way. For any transformation of discipleship to be effective, we simply *must go* someplace outside of our comfort zone. We believe that when Jesus told us to go into all ends of the world, part of that direction was to ensure that we simply couldn't stay in any area of limited growth or understanding. The "going" part of a DiscipleTrip is the part that is transformative. That's our intention here; no matter where your DiscipleTrip actually takes you, geographically.

One last disclaimer, before we embark. The content of your personal DiscipleTrip is not within these pages. It has already been created and determined from before you were born. We're hoping this book acts as the travel companion for your Trip. Your job is to be willing to go, seek, and discover the adventure that is ready and waiting for you, personally. And we're ready to "go" alongside you. It's literally the adventure of your life.

Whether or not you are planning an actual trip or simply walking through life with Jesus and the company of others in your own home, workplace, or coffee shop, I pray that this endeavor will be as transformative for you as it has been for me. It certainly was transformative for those who walked with Jesus on the dirt path some 2,000 years ago. As the ancient rabbinical admonition goes, "may you be covered in the dust of your Rabbi."

The great commission wasn't meant to create travelers; it was meant to make disciples. It was meant to make us understand that we are to create disciples as we are going – wherever we are going. Adventure isn't just out there. It's right here. If you are a follower of Christ, you have been invited to live the ultimate adventure.

- Joey Cook

My DiscipleTrip story is a day-to-day submission to crown Jesus king while loving on others and leading them to His relentless love. Through a spirit of vulnerability and community with others, grace has awakened in my soul. In this new understanding of discipleship, I have been able to meet people where they are and see their brokenness as a tool to make Jesus, king, not a tool to teach them how to be better. The adventure is all around us; it's right now with your coworkers, children, the waitress at your favorite restaurant, and the mom at the park. Discipleship opportunities are all around. No need to go on an adventure when the adventure of watching someone grow in Christ is in your backyard.

- Syndal Cook

Chapter 1: An Unexpected Adventure

WITHOUT A DOUBT, IT WAS THE CRAZIEST 12-HOUR PERIOD OF MY LIFE, and six of it had been spent sleeping. It was a gorgeous evening in the Pacific Northwest. As the shadows lengthened, light burst through every crack and crevice between trees and buildings on the campus of Evergreen State University in West Olympia, Washington. We had been told that this was the most liberal college in the United States, but for a kid from the south, graduating from college with a music or theatre degree was a left-wing activity. After spending some time with our new friend Rory, I had a better understanding of what they meant.

A handful of my closest friends and I met Rory while walking through a mid-afternoon tour of the college. He was reciting poetry over, what at least seemed to be, random strums on the guitar. Afterwards, we applauded his rather creative prose. He then bowed in thankfulness and offered the guitar to one of my adventure buddies, Lane Long. Lane and I had been walking through life for quite some time at this point. (Our relationship, written from his perspective, is included later in the chapter, "Stories from the Road.") Lane immediately thumbed out a new worship song that we had been singing as a part of the nightly program associated with our mission. That mission, "City Reach," was, essentially, a good deeds and good news project that included 200 or so college students who would descend on a city hoping to reach residents with the life-changing message of Jesus. As we began to dialogue with our new friend, we discovered that Rory was homeless, although that was not how he described it. In his words, Rory's home was the forest. This came as quite a surprise to many of us who only spent time in the woods when we were mountain biking, hiking, hunting, or camping. Evidently, this was pretty normal protocol for local students. "70% of the campus lives in these woods," Rory informed us. "Yeah, it's beautiful out there. Wanna eat dinner and go out there with me tonight?"

We had prayed that God would open up opportunities to connect and share the Good News of Jesus with people at Evergreen College. This opportunity was not quite what we expected, but I was blessed enough to be in the company of guys who are not afraid to take risks. The crew I came with was dedicated and committed to knowing that we were there with purpose. It seemed, now, as though Rory might have been a big part in that purpose.

"Yes, but only after our gathering," we told Rory. "Gathering?" Rory asked. "Yes, we follow Jesus together. Tonight, we are going to share some stories of today's service projects and celebrate through music, as well as learn more about God and the life that he has called us to lead from the Bible," I explained. "Can I come?" Rory asked. "Of course," we collectively stated. To our delight, Rory said that he would like to follow this same Jesus that we follow, who motivates us to serve others. On a street curb after our gathering, Rory confessed his sin and trusted Jesus as his new Lord and Savior.

"Ready to go to the woods?"

"As ready as we'll ever be," my friend Carson replied. "We'll get our hammocks!"

On the way into the woods, Rory told us that the experience would be more meaningful if we don't turn on our flashlights, but rather rely on the light of the moon. "Your eyes will adjust," he said. He was right. Our eyes adjusted to the darkness and the path began to take shape. A few hundred yards into our late-night forest hike, Rory stopped our caravan and wrapped his arms around a large Cyprus tree. "If you hold it for eight seconds, your body will release the same amount of endorphins as it does while hugging another human." The eyeballs of all five men began to bounce back and forth as we contemplated our next move.

I suppose this was the moment I officially became a tree hugger ... along with the rest of the guys.

A half mile or so later, we noticed a faint glow in the distance. As we neared what we came to realize was a campfire, mystery ensued. We quickly noticed that, although there were logs laid down to provide fireside seating, no one was present on them.

"Hello..." Rory spoke into the vast span of trees surrounding the trailhead. "Hello?"

"Are you cops?" a voice echoed back.

"Do I look like a cop?" This clever comeback was well-spoken, given the fact that Rory stood about 5'10 with wavy red hair that made its way past his chin, just shy of his shoulders, all around his ears. It was a pretty safe bet that Rory hadn't bathed in quite some time. The smell that hovered around his stick-figure frame would have classified him as "a man of nature" for sure. His answer seemed to satisfy the request of the mystery man. We followed him, as he slowly entered the scene, and proceeded to sit at the fire in silence.

The next few moments could accurately be described as "awkward silence." But the black haired, slightly unkempt man, who appeared to be somewhere in his early thirties, broke the silence. "My name's Righteous," he said in a manner that matched his mysterious entrance.

"Hi Righteous, I'm Rory," our tour guide stated as we all sat wedged somewhere between fear and amazement at the scene that had continued to unfold before us.

"Sorry about asking you if you were cops. I escaped from the city and you just can't be too sure these days," Righteous said.

You're telling me, I thought to myself, hoping that I had not mistakenly stated the phrase out loud. We continued the odd introductions around the fire; "Aaron, Dakota, Carson, Lane, Joey." One at a time, each just as uncomfortable as the next.

"Hey, have you guys ever walked on coals?" Rory broke the silence. It was another priceless moment of us all eyeballing one another with raised eyebrows, sounding a unanimous "No…" In the same unexpected pace of our adventure, we would now be presented with the opportunity. As Rory began to drag red hot remnants of what was once large logs, he tried to reassure us that this was a great idea and that "people do it all the time and don't get hurt." This is a line I have heard before; even used to bring others into precarious situations that might later be worth telling stories about.

Rory went first. His bony and pale feet softly stepped, one after the other, until he reached approximately 12 feet to the other side. Once across, he let out a shriek of victory. His smile seemed to wrap from ear to ear. "You just gotta commit," he said. "And never stop moving." Our group of newbies hesitated to form the line. But, after a minute, I knew what I had to do. "Let's do this," I said, and I immediately made my way across the smoldering coals. "Whew! That was a rush! Now I get it. It never made sense before this moment, but now it does." Slowly, but surely, nearly half of the group reluctantly made their way across. Then, I decided to cross again. Turns out, the second trip wasn't nearly as efficient as the first. Somehow, a coal pressed its way into the small space between my fourth and pinky toes, immediately creating a blister on a very tender spot underfoot. "Still worth it," I thought to myself.

Certain that nothing was going to top this adrenaline-infused event, we were quick to find out we were wrong. After hanging a bit longer at Righteous' fire, Rory extended yet another invitation. "Have you ever swam with bio-luminescent bacteria?" Once again, the group found consensus in not having experienced this particular activity.

"It's cool," Rory said. "Just watch."

Just then, he reached down and picked up a rock and flung it into the dark gap in the trees, into what we could only perceive as some type of body of water, lit by the reflection of the moon. Immediately at the point of impact, a bright, neon green circle appeared at the center ripple of the waters and made its way gently outward until the water returned to a smooth black layer.

"They give off a glow, when irritated," Rory informed his new friend group. "Come on, it's even better when you are in the water!"

About that time, Rory began to strip down to his tighty whities. He then jumped in the water and we watched, in childlike wonder, as the bacteria put off a brilliant glow all around him. He assured us that the water felt great. That was just enough to convince the rest of us to join him in this late-night swim, which was beginning to feel like a euphoric dream. Between his convincing and my foot hurting from the fire-walk it actually started to seem like a good strategy to cool it down. As I reflect on this experience, four years later, those ten minutes still feel like a distant fairy tale. We laughed and played like little children, giddy with excitement and wonder. We were amazed at what we were getting to take part in. It was as if we were living out a scene that you'd only see in some cool sci-fi movie.

After our swim, we got dressed and decided to warm ourselves by the fire for a bit. We shared a few snacks that we had thrown in a bag before we set out that evening. After putting some food in our bellies, we said our goodbyes to Righteous. Rory told us that we would be sleeping "just up the hill" from the fire and that we should get going in order to set up our hammocks and get a good night's rest. Little did we know that the "hill" that Rory had referred to was more like a cliff. As we scaled it in the pitch dark, only lit by the light of the moon, we clung to tree roots, stepped on each other's shoulders, and even clawed in the dirt in order to get to our cliff-top "campsite." Once at the top, we found a grove of trees that with some creative engineering, would serve as our anchor points for the hammocks. Hours later, what we observed at sunrise made all of the effort worthwhile.

As the light peeked over the edge of my hammock, I forced a squint and peered at what the darkness had engulfed and hidden from us the night before. The hammocks bordered a ridge on the bluff of the Puget Sound. There was not one puff of wind. Only a single boat, with a sail hoisted high in the air, sat motionless on the bay. The edge of the cliff provided us a bird's eye view of the most spectacular scene my eyes have ever seen. The reflection of the boat on the water was as clear as the boat itself. The radiant reds, yellows, and oranges, provided by the first glimpse of the top half of the morning sun, seemed to swallow the Earth, wrapping my fellow travelers and I in warmth and beauty; a pleasant alarm clock, indeed. My attention then turned behind me, as I heard the strumming of a well-tuned guitar. I made my way out of the suspended cocoon and toward the fire to hear what Rory was playing at the warm edge of our newly lit campfire; which was complete with the freshest sticks and logs around. "How did you light this fire?" I asked Rory. "I made my way down the hill this morning and took a coal from Righteous' fire in order to start ours this morning. I guess you could say that it's simply a metaphor that speaks to what Jesus has done in my heart as a result of meeting you guys." Wow. I sat in amazement as the wonder continued to accumulate in my own heart.

"One of the people in your group gave me this Bible and I'm really enjoying it. Do you want to read with me?" Rory then read from one of the Gospels for a bit and handed the book to me. I continued where he left off. Together, we read the story of the farmer scattering seed, at the fire that he built by bringing a coal up from the fire of a friend. And as he read, my heart was blazing. *This is as good as life can be on this side of eternity*, I thought to myself. Before long, everyone was awake; sitting around the fire, singing songs to Jesus. We sang about His mercy and His grace. We sang about His forgiveness and His love. Then we wrote a song about our experience that went something like this:

"Have you ever walked on a bed of coals?

Have you ever swam with neon fish as they glow?

Have you ever hugged a tree or woke up on a beautiful sea?"

The song was a proclamation of the evening that we spent making memories with our new friend. It was a song about taking risks and trying new things. It was a song of faith; the kind of faith that leaps before looking or stands headlong in the face of fear, for a pursuit of the unknown. That evening, Rory experienced Jesus, and so did we. It was an experience that marked us and continues to be influential to this day.

In the epic 80's movie, *Stand by Me*, a group of boys have the experience of a lifetime. They experience true freedom, fear, laughter, and even death. Once they return, something is different. They can't put their finger on it, but they know they will never be the same. After we sang, we walked back to Evergreen State University having been infused with wonder, awe, and a sense of accomplishment. Stories about that night still never quite do it justice.

This, my friend, is one of the many stories I've collected as I've embarked on my own DiscipleTrip; the experience of my lifetime. Although this publication will be available to many, it has been my desire to write it as a very intimate, personal reflection of what it means to have discipleship done right; and what it means to have been there, (on the receiving end), when discipleship fails. Unfortunately, even with the best intentions, and the development of new programs and strategies for making disciples, many of us continue to participate in failed discipleship. We are missing the mark because we are missing the basics.

That's the mission of what you now hold in your hands. We want to take you away so that you can get a new perspective on the basics of raw, real life, following Jesus. We want to take you away from your ideas of ministry, of serving and of structured discipleship efforts. This trip isn't about going on a trip across the world and wearing matching t-shirts with 20 others from your local church, but rather about seeing ourselves as missionaries in the every day.

We are going to come undone; be rebuilt and refocused. The rebuild requires some reflection, and it may require some demolition. But the power of a changed life is the most effective tool of any believer.

So come with me, my brother or sister. I've got some bruises to show you from my trips, but I can help you avoid some of your own. I've had some great views along the way, but God is painting and preparing new ones for both of us to see. Let's get ready to live the adventure.

Chapter 2: The Road Behind

LET ME TAKE A MOMENT and welcome you on this DiscipleTrip. I'm hoping this is not your first one, but it may be different from any that you have ever taken before. We're about to head down the raw and barefoot, dirt path that Jesus took with His own disciples. So, let's get a good start by figuring out where we are, here, at the beginning.

Sometimes, display maps at a museum or park will have an indicator to show you, "You are here." Aren't they helpful? Life seems like it would be a lot simpler if we had those to point out where we are in our development. Sometimes, we need to seek them out ourselves.

The Importance of an Honest Start

Let's be real. An honest start is the critical first step of the journey. Consider showing up to the airport and trying to lie about your identity to get onto a flight. Not only will you likely end up in jail, it's highly doubtful you'll be on the plane to your desired destination as it's taking off. Perhaps a circumstance that we'd be more likely to encounter? You meet someone online and begin talking only to find out that their online picture doesn't match their actual appearance. Anything that starts off on a false note is unlikely to succeed. If we're going to build a house, the last thing we want is a foundation of sand (Matt 7:26). We must proceed from a place of honesty on this first leg of the journey.

Before the wheels leave our driveway, we have to be honest about who we are. We're going to jump right in and get down to business. Let's take a moment of personal inventory now.

- Who is Jesus to you?
- Is He truly your Lord?
- Does He have control over your heart, will and ambitions?
- Do you have a genuine interest in following His command to make disciples?
- Are you looking to lead a DiscipleTrip as a way of fulfilling some need for value and affirmation from others?
- What are the apps on the home screen of your phone? What would this have to do with DiscipleTrip?

By the way, it's ok if we don't all know what it means to make disciples, or how to do that. A large part of DiscipleTrip is learning about what that looks like in real life. For now, let's continue our inventory.

Passport Requirements

Just like in traveling, our passport identifies us and where we come from. In fact, in this world, it's impossible to know our true identity, unless we know where we came from. This is not a subjective matter. We all came from the same source, it's just a matter of whether we identify with it or not.

According to the Word of God, the Bible, we all were made in His image (Gen 1:27), as His carefully made creation (Psalm 139:14), with a purpose and plan from before we were born (Jer 1:5, Eph 2:10). Not one single cell or hair on us has been by mistake or is unaccounted for (Luke 12:7). He knows every part of our story from the beginning to the end (Psalm 139: 1-16). In fact, He's been in every part of each of our stories, whether we knew it or not (1 Cor 8:6, 1 Cor 12:6). He even knew that we'd intersect on these very pages, at this moment.

"He" is the Creator of the Universe, of all things, seen and unseen (Col 1:16). But even with all the things He's created, He longs to be with us; not within a religious ritual, but within our hearts, and certainly within our life. He longs to know us intimately, so as to prove that His love can go into every part of our being, all of our interaction, our mind and our journey on this earth… and redeem it. In fact, He was so determined that we know that, that He sacrificed His only Son to prove it (John 3:16).

Despite that unfathomable sacrifice, He is still willing to let us decide whether we want Him or not. Our identity for eternity rests on this choice. And if we don't actively make the choice to identify with Him, the default is that we don't get to move into His presence, in Heaven, at the end of this life.

The Bible says there are two requirements to getting our "passport" into the only perfect destination, where we will be face to face, in His presence, in Heaven. We must:

- ✓ confess with our mouth that Jesus is Lord and
- ✓ believe in our heart that God raised Him from the dead (Romans 10:9).

If you have any doubts about these two things, you are not alone. Most current "passport holders" have journeyed through doubt and may still face temptation in that area. Here's where stuff gets real.

Satan, also known as "the god of this world" (2 Cor 4:4), would like us to think that this is all there is because he wants to cheat us. This world, and all of its sin, is as good as it gets for him. His plan is that we remain so focused on this world and our desire to belong to it (1 John 2:15-17) that once we die, we stay in death. Our bodies die here, and with our bodies, so do our chances for eternal life in bliss. So, believer ("passport holder"), or non-believer, Satan would like for us to think that this is the better destination. In fact, he's so set on us thinking that way that he will devote time throughout our entire lifespan to trying to cheat and deceive us, even with the distraction of non-decision, out of the other option to inherit the Kingdom as co-heirs (Romans 8:17). Ever heard the saying, "misery loves company?" As much as he hates us, Satan would rather not be alone in his great downfall.

The other option, of course, is Heaven. No, this is not some cheesy description of us floating on clouds and eating unlimited cookies. In fact, the reality is that Heaven is a "bliss" beyond anything that our human mind can comprehend, and the Bible says that our bodies, these bodies, cannot live in the presence of that magnificence (Exo 33:20). Simply put, we don't even have the capacity to survive the description of how awesome it really is. It is, quite literally, mind-blowing.

So, we have two choices for destination after this life. The first is Heaven, where we have pre-determined beforehand to identify with our Creator, secure our "passport," and live in eternity with Him, undeservedly. Or we can choose to opt-out, make no decision at all, or, simply put, not get to it in time. That destination, whether we intended or not, is separation from our Creator for eternity; also known as Hell.

Now it's pretty easy for us to know when we've "fulfilled" the worldly travel passport requirements because we get the hardcopy passport in hand. With Jesus, our passport is much, much more dynamic. If we truly confess with our mouth that Jesus is Lord and believe that God raised Him from the dead (Romans 10:9), our "passport" is that the Holy Spirit, which is God Himself in Spirit form, comes to take up residence in our heart. Because Matthew 25:31-46 says that God will separate all people into two groups at judgement, one group with the Holy Spirit living inside of them, and the other group of those without, the Holy Spirit is the one to secure our passage into Heaven. We cannot take this lightly. This life is really not that long. Heaven is real. Hell is real. One of them is our next destination.

Is a "passport," in this case, our reference to the Holy Spirit and a choice of salvation, a requirement for a DiscipleTrip? No, friend. All are invited. Just like the Creator reflects, we are each allowed our own choice. But life with Jesus? It's *life*. And it's awesome. It's the ultimate, forever passport – totally free to you. The final destination is, literally, perfection; and every step before that is planned with precision, to get you there.

Sometimes, we need to think about *where* we've been and what *could have* been, to see that properly.

MAPPING THE ROAD BEHIND

Often, when someone is about to embark on a trip, they carefully map the road ahead. For our trip, though, we're going to make sure we have an appropriate view of the road behind, first. What's happened behind us will impact what's about to happen in front of us.

In Matthew 7: 3-5, Jesus talks about examining ourselves honestly:

WHY DO YOU LOOK AT THE SPECK OF SAWDUST IN YOUR BROTHER'S EYE AND PAY NO ATTENTION TO THE PLANK IN YOUR OWN EYE? HOW CAN YOU SAY TO YOUR BROTHER, 'LET ME TAKE THE SPECK OUT OF YOUR EYE,' WHEN ALL THE TIME THERE IS A PLANK IN YOUR OWN EYE? YOU HYPOCRITE, FIRST TAKE THE PLANK OUT OF YOUR OWN EYE, AND THEN YOU WILL SEE CLEARLY TO REMOVE THE SPECK FROM YOUR BROTHER'S EYE.

According to the Scripture, we are to take a close look in the mirror before we can help others appropriately. Self-reflection for the sole purpose of focusing on ourselves, though, is not wise and can be a slippery slope into self-indulgence or the all-popular "pity-party." That is not our purpose here.

Yet to take an honest start, let's do an exercise in self-reflection as a means to see where we are in Christ, what He's done in our lives, and how we can use this in our DiscipleTrip. Check out the "Bonus Challenge" at the end of this chapter to get started.

By the way, remember when we asked what apps are on the home screen of your phone? The Bible says, where your treasure is, there your heart will be also. (Matt

6:21). Where we spend our time, is where our interests really lie. Your phone's home screen reveals a lot about what you spend the most time with. Are those aligned with the journey you're about to take?

Chapter 3: Adventure Awaits

The kingdom of heaven is like treasure hidden in a field, which a man found and covered up. Then in his joy he goes and sells all that he has and buys that field. (Matthew 13:44)

I T IS 3:37 A.M. AND, FOR SOME REASON, the familiar sound of the horn, from the nightly train that runs through the heart of our city, takes me back to dull roar of the local insects inhabiting the brushy plains of the Magangani village.

The year was 2010. I had traveled across the globe with two friends from my hometown of Mountain View, Arkansas. Mike was a small-town contractor of new homes and Matt sold cars as a part of the family business. We were in the fifth day of a two-week trip to East Kenya, Africa, not far from the Indian

Ocean. We had spent the better part of the week working with the locals, building thatched-roof, open air structures that would provide shelter from the intense rays from the African sun; one that I had never before experienced, as I had never been as close to the equator as I was on this trip. The missionary that we were serving told Matt, Mike, and myself that we needed to consume at least two gallons of water, per day, while weaving the water-soaked vines through palm leaf rooves. The thermometer read 120 degrees Fahrenheit in the shade where I sat. I was able to work for ten minutes at a time, in the sun. Then, in order to avoid becoming overheated, I would take a ten-minute rest. It was such a different pace for me although it didn't seem to faze the locals too much. We used long shafts of steel, approximately six feet in length to crush the dried coral around the bases of the poles that would serve as the pillars to hold the roof. Those were long and hard days of work. But this fifth day had been different.

Our local missionary connection was named James Taylor. No, he was not the famous singer, but he did have soul, and lots of it! He had been working among the remote villages along the eastern seaboard for the better part of the last decade. He possessed a near mastery of the Swahili language of the natives. As we loaded the Land Rover at his family's home one morning, he pointed to the Japanese-manufactured overland motorcycle that he used to access even more remote areas of the country. James told us of the alligator-infested river that they would cross, in a hand-carved canoe, motorcycle and all, after a three-hour ride that placed them squarely under a bramble tree. There the men of the local village would huddle around a solar-powered tape player called "the proclaimer." The Proclaimer would echo out Jesus' words recorded in the book of John from the New Testament; a treasure, serving as the narrative driving their own faith experiences. They discussed what it meant to be a follower of this man, named Jesus, and how His teaching impacted the way they lived their lives and the conversations they now had with their family and friends. Yes, life in Africa was certainly much different than I had experienced in the Western Hemisphere.

After packing, we set out for safari. It was a two-and-a-half-hour drive to this particular national park. I wish you could have seen the potholes on this road, some of which seemed as large as a VW Beetle. We eventually made it to the front entrance, paid our entry fee and set out in the open plains to experience a day I will never forget. We rode near the edge of rivers, where the wild hippos observed us; eyes gleaming from just above the surface of the water. We watched the large herds of zebras roam the vast fields. We turned one corner and waited, patiently, as a family of elephants crossed the dirt road past the hood of our car. We watched the giraffes stretch their long, spotted necks to eat leaves from the trees. We shared our food with the wild monkeys who watched us eat - with nervous anticipation in the presence of their rare, white-faced guests. But my favorite animal, in all of the safari, was the lion. James informed us that he had seen lions on only one-fourth of his safaris, and this was our lucky day. Because of the overcasting clouds, it felt much cooler on this fifth day of the trip. In fact, the temperature had dipped to a beautiful and dry 80 degrees. It was so nice, that I ended up riding shirtless on top of the Land Rover Defender's roof rack. I found it much easier to take pictures, and even film, from this vantage point. What was more difficult, however, was dealing with the third-degree sunburn that occurred as a result.

You can imagine my surprise when the elusive "king of the jungle" crossed the road ahead of us, and James shouted out of his open window, "Hold on, we are going off-road to chase the lion!"

Now, you're probably going to think that this next scene sounds a little crazy, and looking back on the scenario, I would completely agree with you. As we navigated from the dirt road to an off-road terrain, I stood upright on the roof rack, in order to see over the bramble bush and capture any lion footage from the highest perspective possible. My background in skateboarding, wakeboarding, and snowboarding helped in maintaining my balance, at a low speed of course, while roof-surfing the safari.

As I stood on the Defender, camera in hand, James carefully navigated the terrain in efforts to help me get footage of the wild beast. "What if he turns around and sees me?" I asked James. "Then drop the camera and get the heck in the window as fast as you can," James replied. We never did get close enough to capture that perfect National Geographic photo submission, but the experience will go down as one of the most adrenaline-infused energy rushes of my life!

Later, on our way to the village of Magangani, I noticed that we were no longer driving on roads. There was only a single, beaten down path that the villagers used to walk around their little community. Kids began to huddle around the vehicle as we progressed down the trail. They were laughing and singing and pointing and shouting. It was clear that they recognized James and the vehicle that we were driving. We arrived at our destination and I was captivated by the scene unfolding around us; a woman sweeping the dirt outside her mud hut with a homemade broom, a couple of men emerging from their dwelling to greet James, free range chickens running wildly around the homes, and many neighborhood children grinning from ear to ear. One boy talked to me while James translated. "You are showing the film of the man who died on the tree tonight?" "Yes," we replied. Within thirty minutes, what seemed to be only an SUV had transitioned into a mobile theatre; complete with a movie screen, projector, and speakers - all powered by the on-board battery. After the movie, we held a discussion and answered questions from many people in the village, both young and old. That evening, we had personal conversations, through the help of a translator, with half a dozen local villagers who decided to trust in Jesus as their Lord and Savior.

We were then invited into one of the mud huts for a dinner under the flickering light of a single candle. The host of the dinner earned a living by working at a meat-processing facility. So, there, perched right on top of our sticky rice, was a small pile of "food" featuring the main course: cross sections of goat intestines. They looked like giant spaghetti-O's staring us right in the face. And we were instructed that there was no need for chewing; the intestines were so tough that they refused to break down. I suppose that is sort of the nature of intestines, right? As any good friend would do, I shoveled my entrée onto the top of my friend Mike's rice every time he wasn't looking. As my plate cleared, our host would offer me more. I would gladly receive it, as is customary as a sign of appreciation, and then repeat the process of laundering intestines. I would also occasionally shame Mike, in jest of course, for not "cleaning his plate" like he would normally do back home. No one noticed.

Near the end of our meal, the host's cell phone beeped. To this day, I still have no idea how people living in third world cultures have such access to technology. Regardless, we could all tell that the phone call immediately shifted the mood to something urgent. The host mumbled a few Swahilian words to James, and exited the mud hut. James followed, then us. As we made our way away from the candlelit dinner, I asked the men what we were doing. "A man was just caught cutting down another man's fruit tree and we are going to save his life," James said. "What?" I anxiously muttered. "In this culture, such a crime is worthy of death. If we don't get there soon, they will bind him in a tire and set it on fire; that is the law of the land." To this day, I can't think of a time in my life where I have felt more panic than this midnight romp through, what I was convinced, was a viper-laden field of waist-high grass, buzzing with the sound of insects and wildlife. The phone rang again. We slowed our jog. The host took the call and relayed the message to James. The man had been forgiven and released. It cost the culprit one of his own chickens and an indefinite probation; both high costs for a resident of Magangani, but also a truce that saved the man's life. Crisis averted. We returned to our place of stay for the night.

Just before falling asleep in our tent, I decided to confess "project goat intestines" to my friends. We shared an explosive outburst of shock and a hard belly laugh that followed, one that probably raised some eyebrows in the African village that night.

I woke up to missionary James' hand on my shoulder. "Get up," he said. "We have to get out of here." There was panic in his voice. "Ok, ok," I said in utter shock, having been fast asleep 30 seconds prior. "What's going on?" "The village is in an uproar. They found a bag with condoms inside and believe the white men have come to our village to have relations with their women!" My body instantly began to shake all over as sheer panic struck deep into the recesses of my heart. "I, I, I didn't mean anything by it, I promise!" I said. "I found a dispenser in the bathroom of the national park and wanted to take a few of them home as a souvenir to show my wife. I thought they were cool because it was all written in Swahili," I rambled on as I simultaneously became emotional at the thought of all I had ruined. As I started to cry, a huge smile came across James' face. "I'm kidding, here's your bag," he said as he handled me the camel back hydration pack that I had strapped to the roof rack on the top of the Land Rover. "But Mike said to eat your own goat intestines next time." I immediately regained the feeling in my face and limbs as I realized it was all a prank – a really, really, good prank.

We left Kenya a few days later. I was still sunburned from the safari adventure, exhausted from the lack of sleep, and forever changed by the whole experience. Looking back, I realized the whole process marked me. I saw a group of people who possessed next to nothing, but without complaint. It was clear that the churches that we had joined knew Jesus, and that was all they needed. After a few days in the company of Jesus and my friends, I realized that much of the stuff that I thought mattered so much, ended up not being that important after all. After worshipping with some of the happiest people I'd ever met, witnessing firsthand their faces as they heard the word of God - some for the very first time – and doing it all without the comforts of my modern world, I realized that the mission trip just might have been primarily about my own transformation.

This, my friend, is the adventure that awaits you. You might not be literally transported to the other end of the world to chase an actual lion, but you may find that the adventure God takes you on has just as much, if not more, to do with your transformation, than that of the company who joins you. Transformation, in God's eyes, requires no shift in geography. But it is always an adventure.

WE INTERRUPT THIS MESSAGE FOR A QUICK APOLOGY

I need to apologize. Not just for myself, but for pastors like me who have made the Gospel of Jesus out to be a safe endeavor. Why the apology? Because following Jesus has always had an element of risk involved. We have somehow fit Christianity in America into a safe and secure suburban context in a way that Jesus never intended.

In fact, according to a study done just a few years ago, Christians are considered the "most persecuted group in the world."[1]

We are incredibly blessed in this country to not currently experience the level of Christian persecution that much of the rest of the world is facing. Yet the atmosphere is changing and a thorough reading of the Bible points to the fact that it will get worse until Jesus comes back. When we talk about adventure in this book, and on our actual DiscipleTrip, we hope it will be one of fun adventures where everyone comes out laughing. Yet, as Christians, we need to understand that the enemy does not want us discipling one another. Part of your preparation for a DiscipleTrip is that you must armor up. This is not just about bumps or flat tires along the road. And the primary danger isn't the safari that you may or may not take. This is about an army within the Spiritual realm that is going to be lined up along the road ready to sabotage you at every turn. And that's not an analogy. We'll talk more about this later.

AND WE'RE BACK

Coming back to pure adventure, we believe that Jesus wants us to take a look at Him differently than we may have in the past. We're so used to looking at Him as the guy hanging lifeless on the cross, that we forget that this is the guy who walked on water and boldly went into the synagogue and threw over the tables of the merchants, as the disciples observed in shock. There was nothing boring or unadventurous about the man who raised people to life, restored eyesight out

---

[1] https://www.gatestoneinstitute.org/4365/christians-most-persecuted

of a mud salve, and who only had to speak to the waves and the wind for them to respond immediately. And that's the guy we're following here.

When Jesus gathered His ragtag followers on the beach in Galilee, He did so by inviting them on a fishing trip. Not a sit-by-the-lake kind of afternoon, where you sip iced-tea and watch the sunset, as your pole sits lazily leaned up to your lawn chair; but the kind of open water, deep sea venture where you are likely to hook a shark and enter into the fight of a lifetime with your pole in hand. The kind of catch that, *if* you were to land the fish in the boat, you would do so drenched in sweat, and provided with quite the story to tell. It would be the kind of fish-wrangling that might just leave you out of breath, with a smile on your face.

You see, living the Gospel of Jesus is a die-to-self activity that takes us out of our comfort zone and into the adventure of the great unknown; one of undeniable transformation. Luckily, Jesus did not invite us to embark on such a fishing trip alone. Not only did He promise to go in front of us, but He promised to go with us and to even cover our backs with the Holy Spirit (Exo 14:19). We are not solo practitioners in this grand experiment, but teammates with others that He has also recruited to the team. We fool ourselves if we somehow believe that following Jesus, this "Christianity" if you will, is a solo sport. Rather, we are to enlist comrades to travel with. But camaraderie cannot be had simply by playing on the same team. It comes through a deeper, more meaningful bond.

On our DiscipleTrip, we are likely to form new friendships, even with those we don't expect. However, DiscipleTrip is not just a friendship building exercise. It is a journey with Jesus in the company of friends. My friend, Alan Hirsch, uses the word "communitas" to describe this shared mission. Communitas is community with purpose. The camaraderie that is formed in this shared mission becomes a true bond that breaks down walls, open hearts and minds, and binds men and women together in a way that only Jesus can. Are you ready to embark on such an adventure?

WHY A DISCIPLETRIP?

Simply put, because we (humans) were made for "action adventure!" The command to "go" into all the nations, involves encountering things, people and experiences that may or may not be within our usual comfortable home setting. We weren't made to withdraw into our own worlds. We were made to go out, into His – and not to go it alone!

We hear the title of "Action/Adventure" as a genre for books, movies and games. But DiscipleTrip is action *plus* adventure. The biggest failure of the Christian walk is to detach understanding from action. Once you "get" who He is and what He's done for you, there simply is no more withdrawing or choice for inactivity. With your understanding of who Christ is, the call is to take action. That action incorporates all of the instruction in our ultimate guidebook – the Bible. If you don't know where to start, simply go with the top two commandments, as Jesus references (Matt 37:40); love Him with everything and love others as yourself. These are our primary actions that influence the whole adventure!

We can't go out only looking for adventure, either. The action is critical, and it will bring the adventure. There has to be purpose in the journey. The purpose of the DiscipleTrip is to allow the space for "going out" into something outside of our own regular world to encounter God in new ways and to take action to allow others to do the same. The amazing thing about a true DiscipleTrip is that this doesn't actually mean that you have to leave your driveway. You just need to be willing to take whatever action Jesus leads you to take and be signed up for the adventure that follows. The command "go" actually means *as we go*. And sometimes, the adventure takes place in the "going" between your own bedroom and kitchen.

The adventure has to be purely for God's glory, and it simply cannot be if we are resistant to participating with our own action. We must do the action, in order to have the adventure. The first and most important action is always submitting to the Holy Spirit's leading. Does that mean you'll be swinging from vines in the jungle or cruising with alligators in the Amazon? Well, if He wants that, then yes. Does it always look like that though? Not exactly.

Truthfully, I sometimes crave more adventure like this! With young children at home, I sometimes wonder if they think that following Jesus produces a monotonous, exhausting life. They often see their parents go through the daily grind and their routines and look quite exhausted by the end of the day. Could we do better to exhibit joy in the journey of raising them? Certainly. But we are human, and even though we sincerely try to steward well all that is in front of us, the journey from their perspective might not look all that enticing or exciting as we collapse on the couch at the end of the day.

There's never a time where my spouse and I choose to just not come home to tend to the kids and the laundry because we are "going on an adventure for Jesus." We don't ever miss picking them up from school because we were "white-water rafting for Jesus." We want to be clear. DiscipleTrip is not an excuse to leave the adventure God has currently got us on! And believe me, raising another human being is the most intense DiscipleTrip adventure. DiscipleTrip is never an excuse to intentionally place anyone else in harm's way because you leave a post of responsibility that He's called you to. DiscipleTrip, in fact, is a purposeful decision of action to put them all, not in harm's way, but in God's way. And when we do that properly, that's where the adventure comes in.

TREASURE SEEKING

As a child, I would sit at the kitchen counter and work cereal box puzzles with my brother, Justin. We would circle the hidden words, find what's wrong with the picture below, and trace our way back from the destination to the start in order to finish the maze. Like most other kids, we would pick the marshmallows from Lucky Charms and leave the rest of those tasteless pieces to sit lonely in the milk. We watched Skittles commercials that taught us to chase the rainbow and follow our dreams. We inherited the American Dream, naturally.

For the majority of my adult life, I have continued to believe that the treasure was located at the end of the rainbow. So, I run. I run. And I run. I learn and I chase. I spin my tires and go on trips. I buy things and I invest. I eat better foods and I sleep in more comfortable beds. I have a bigger house than I used to, and my vehicles are now newer and more dependable. I exercise. I have life insurance and my children have nice shoes. We go on vacation, every year. And, sometimes, twice a year.

As I approach 40, I am beginning to notice that my body is beginning to shape shift, ever so slightly. I have lost my first step on the basketball court. I have visited many of the places that I longed to go as a child. I have lived in several cities and different states. I have dined at the finest restaurants and I have flown first class. I have enjoyed these experiences. And yet somehow, I know that there is more. I finish them unsatisfied. On to the next.

More to experience, more to accomplish. All the while somehow knowing it will not be enough.

If you've never read the book of Ecclesiastes, now is the time to do it. It's not that long, and it's God's Word on this very topic.

King Solomon, the writer, was regarded as the wisest man on earth. But within his human desires, he chased all the things we do – riches, money, women, power and adventure. He confirms that all his pursuits and the wisdom concluding from those pursuits, and even obtaining all of those "treasures," led to nothing. Nothing. No satisfaction, no contentment, no lasting pleasure. He refers to them as "meaningless" and "worthless" throughout the book.

Take a moment and consider this with me. Think of the top four or five "treasures" that you are seeking most out of your life and see if they're among the things that Solomon quotes as having brought true contentment. Did you find what Solomon says?

In Ecclesiastes chapter 3, Solomon says that the only things, out of all of those "treasures" that he had pursued and captured, that brought him pleasure, were the eating, drinking, and working of everyday life. Seriously? The "wisest" man on earth just said that routine, everyday life brought pleasure beyond the "treasures" previously listed? Doesn't that sound like the least exciting adventure ever?

And this, friend, is where our paradigm begins to shift from the temporal to the eternal.

What King Solomon realized, in all of his wisdom, was that the "treasure" we regard on earth, even in all of its shiny glory and fancy packages, still cannot compare with the simple abiding we do with our Savior and in the way He sustains us until we get into His presence. In other words, after all of his experience, wisdom led Solomon to know that the treasure, ultimately, was just living life with the Savior.

Does that mean that we're not to experience life to the fullest, and not to do anything other than work, eat, or drink? Nope. What it means is that if you find your contentment in the everyday abiding, working, eating and drinking with your Savior, then anything else will be an adventure and an experience that can be enjoyed without the deception that it is some kind of treasure that will bring fulfillment. In other words, you will be able to enjoy things for what they are, and not what for what they are not.

The treasure Jesus provides isn't about waiting to get to the end of a thing. Not to sound cliché, but He really is the treasure. You don't even have to journey out to get it either.

That is what He is offering to me, to you, to us, today. He is offering Himself. He is offering His presence. In Him, striving ceases. In Him, we find life and joy and peace. In Him, our hearts can find contentment. When you and I find that Jesus is all we have ever wanted, all we have ever needed, it is then that our wandering hearts can rest. We can enjoy the feast that He has prepared for His children and all the other adventure that comes along with it.

Jesus *is the treasure* worth selling everything for (Matt 13:44).

The journey is the destination! Buckle up. We're heading out soon.

Chapter 4: Departure Point

We may set out with a clean heart to partake in our DiscipleTrip, but what do our surroundings look like at the departure point?

We cannot lead anyone else if we have left a mess at home. Paul tells Timothy:

> FOR IF A MAN CANNOT MANAGE HIS OWN HOUSEHOLD, HOW CAN HE TAKE CARE OF GOD'S CHURCH? (1 TIM 3:5 NLT)

No matter how much we may want to go on a DiscipleTrip outside the home, the first and most important one we take is the one that doesn't require any travel. Adventure is here! This is very much like the personal inventory we looked at in the first chapter. Before departing, we have to take a true inventory of what our own household looks like. Let's consider these questions:

- Do the members of our household understand what discipleship is or why we should do it?

- Do the members of our household disciple one another?

- Who else in our household is involved with discipleship outside of the home?

- Is the Bible the authority for our household?

Does this mean that everyone in our household needs to be walking around quoting Scripture to one another all day? Or that everyone in the household gets excited about Bible study and worship? No. We are all at different places in our journey and God knows each of our hearts. Perhaps we live in a household of non-believers, or perhaps we live alone. As we talked about earlier, self-examination is an important part of your preparation for the trip, so if you live alone, all the more reason to do it. And if you live with a household of non-believers, this is a great opportunity to open up conversation about their willingness to go on an adventure with you.

Yet, we should see fruit being produced from branches (the believers) that are connected to the Vine (the Savior). John, chapter 15, talks about Jesus being the true Vine and the branches being His disciples (us). If we are truly connected to the Vine, we will produce fruit. Matthew 7:16 reinforces that "you will know them by their fruit." We should be able to look around our home and see fruit being harvested by those who claim Him. If we cannot see it, our departure point becomes our journey. We can't leave behind our first priority which is to manage our household well. These are the closest disciples God has placed in our lives and He's waiting to see how we tend to them. Remember, Jesus told Peter that if he loved Him, to tend to His sheep (John 21: 15-19). Tend your sheep.

THE MULTI-GENERATIONAL ADVANTAGE

While you're looking around at your departure point, don't necessarily assume that you are to be the oldest and wisest among the disciples on this trip or that you have to go far to secure the adventure at hand. While your extended family may not be in the same household as you, there is great value in obtaining their advice, support or even presence on your DiscipleTrip!

On a recent camping trip, I took, there were three generations present from the same family. As stories were shared, laughter was had and lessons were reflected upon, discipleship took on new form and shape from the elements that were already present. Sometimes, we do not need a map to find our most valuable resources. Take a look around, and consider what and who surrounds you where you already are.

HOME IS PRIORITY, BUT NOT OUR FIRST LOVE

Home is the starting departure point and also a large part of the destination. Remember, as we tackled in the last chapter, DiscipleTrip is never about leaving anyone in harm's way simply because we are seeking adventure. Home is the first church we serve for Jesus.

However, we serve them because we serve Him. We love because He first loved us. (1 John 4:19)

A LARGE CROWD WAS FOLLOWING JESUS. HE TURNED AROUND AND SAID TO THEM, "IF YOU WANT TO BE MY DISCIPLE, YOU MUST, BY COMPARISON, HATE EVERYONE ELSE—YOUR FATHER AND MOTHER, WIFE AND CHILDREN, BROTHERS AND SISTERS—YES, EVEN YOUR OWN LIFE. OTHERWISE, YOU CANNOT BE MY DISCIPLE. AND IF YOU DO NOT CARRY YOUR OWN CROSS AND FOLLOW ME, YOU CANNOT BE MY DISCIPLE. (LUKE 14:25-27)

We've just heard that we should "love" them and "hate" them – by comparison – so which is it? It's both. If we look at Jesus' two primary commandments, we'll understand why:

> AND YOU MUST LOVE THE LORD YOUR GOD WITH ALL YOUR HEART, ALL
> YOUR SOUL, ALL YOUR MIND, AND ALL YOUR STRENGTH.' THE SECOND IS
> EQUALLY IMPORTANT: 'LOVE YOUR NEIGHBOR AS YOURSELF.' NO OTHER
> COMMANDMENT IS GREATER THAN THESE." (MARK 12:30-31 NLT)

If we love God with everything we have, no other relationship will compare to it. The stark contrast we should experience between our all-consuming love for God and our extension of that love to other humans on earth, connects the comparison of love and hate. Our love for humans, including ourselves, should never be all-consuming, but our love for God should. So, by comparison, we should be so completely in love with the Savior that we would leave all for Him.

The difference in our action comes in when we recognize where God wants us to serve. We need to tend to whatever roles He has placed us in, before we seek out new ones. We need to let the all-consuming love for Him spread out from us, rippling through what is closest to us first, and then extending out.

So, this is what we've established at the departure point, so far:

1. Our departure point is where He's already placed us – at home.
2. Our first mission is to tend to those who He's already placed in our care.

If we've secured those items, let's make sure we have an honest assessment of what else we should consider before we prepare to depart. We count the cost.

COUNTING THE COST

Regardless of who is piling into the car, you can't enter into a DiscipleTrip without accounting for the time, energy, and even money that it will realistically take. The process of counting the cost is faithful stewardship and a critical piece to a successful departure.

So, what does it look like to "count the cost?" Jesus, – of course – says it best.

> BUT DON'T BEGIN UNTIL YOU COUNT THE COST. FOR WHO WOULD BEGIN CONSTRUCTION OF A BUILDING WITHOUT FIRST CALCULATING THE COST TO SEE IF THERE IS ENOUGH MONEY TO FINISH IT? OTHERWISE, YOU MIGHT COMPLETE ONLY THE FOUNDATION BEFORE RUNNING OUT OF MONEY, AND THEN EVERYONE WOULD LAUGH AT YOU. THEY WOULD SAY, 'THERE'S THE PERSON WHO STARTED THAT BUILDING AND COULDN'T AFFORD TO FINISH IT!'
> "OR WHAT KING WOULD GO TO WAR AGAINST ANOTHER KING WITHOUT FIRST SITTING DOWN WITH HIS COUNSELORS TO DISCUSS WHETHER HIS ARMY OF 10,000 COULD DEFEAT THE 20,000 SOLDIERS MARCHING AGAINST HIM? AND IF HE CAN'T, HE WILL SEND A DELEGATION TO DISCUSS TERMS OF PEACE WHILE THE ENEMY IS STILL FAR AWAY. SO YOU CANNOT BECOME MY DISCIPLE WITHOUT GIVING UP EVERYTHING YOU OWN (LUKE 14:28-33 NLT)

Does that mean that you are going to clear out your bank account for a DiscipleTrip and sell everything you own? For most of us, probably not. But let's look at some obvious "costs" involved: time, talent, and treasure.

DISCIPLETRIP REQUIRES A TIME COMMITMENT

How much time does it take? All of it! Jesus said you cannot follow me if you do not carry your cross daily (Luke 9:23). He didn't put a timeline on carrying our cross. And He certainly didn't say to only do it between the hours of 9-5. We don't need to get overwhelmed though; we just need to understand what giving all of our time really means.

It means reprioritizing your life around Kingdom priorities, not man's priorities. This isn't about adding to your already busy life. It isn't about quitting our jobs or ignoring our responsibilities "in the name of Jesus." It simply means doing what you are already doing with a new purpose. I love the way Eugene Peterson puts it in *The Message*:

> SO HERE'S WHAT I WANT YOU TO DO, GOD HELPING YOU: TAKE YOUR
> EVERYDAY, ORDINARY LIFE—YOUR SLEEPING, EATING, GOING-TO-WORK,
> AND WALKING-AROUND LIFE—AND PLACE IT BEFORE GOD AS AN OFFERING.
> (ROMANS 12: 1-2 THE MESSAGE)

I recently heard from a man named Soup Campbell (feel free to Google him) from Memphis, TN, who has lived the majority of his adult life dedicated to the purpose of making disciples. He has literally walked with hundreds of men as they followed Jesus together. Soup says that disciple-making starts in the morning as soon as your feet hit the floor and does not stop until you close your eyes at the end of the evening. Even if we are going on an actual mission trip for a week, or two weeks, our mission doesn't end when we pull back up at home, because the call to make disciples doesn't end until Jesus comes back (Matt 28:18-20). In fact, one of the purposes of this trip is to help us realize that the mission to make disciples continues to all ends of the earth (Acts 1:8); even the ones you are most familiar with.

DISCIPLETRIP REQUIRES AN ENERGY/TALENT COMMITMENT

The time commitment is one that all Trip Mates should make in the same manner; agreeing to devote their attention to the purposes of discipling and growing in Jesus. The energy/talent commitment, though, has a more personal implication.

While we all should be devoting our best energy to disciple-making, that energy may look different for different individuals or circumstances. For instance, some of us have the gift of a lot of energy in the morning, while others have more at night. We should use those specific traits in ways that benefit everyone. So, if you are naturally more energized at night, then plan to devote that energy towards investing in others during that time. If you have great energy as an extrovert, use that to benefit others around you, as well. Plan and commit to using your best energy to create the best circumstances.

Using your talents is also a personal and individual commitment. The Bible says that each of us are given gifts (Rom 12:6) and that they should all be used to benefit the body of Christ. We were each given unique gifts so that, together, we would work as a whole (1 Peter 4:10). Therefore, if you choose not to utilize one of your gifts, you actually hurt the whole, instead of help. Consider the unique gifts God has given you, and consider ahead of time how you can specifically utilize those gifts on the DiscipleTrip to benefit everyone around you. Give freely, with sincere joy and without expectation or a need for recognition.

DiscipleTrip Requires a Treasure Commitment

This is always a touchy subject, even amongst disciples. The truth is, none of what we have belongs to us. It all belongs to Him, so what we're willing to give of "treasure" is really a discussion of what we're willing to give back.

In any journey, we need to eat, have clothes, food, and shelter, each day. The level to which we decide to spend money on those things should always be done prayerfully. God promises to provide for all of our needs as long as we seek first His Kingdom (Matt 6:26-33).

However, there's much to be said for humility. Jesus tells the rich young ruler in Matthew 19 (verses 16-22) that in order to follow Him, he needs to sell all of his belongings. While this may not be our exact calling here, the point is for us not to cling to material things or wealth. Jesus was testing as to whether those things were more important to the young man, and as he walked away depressed by Jesus' advice, it was revealed that they were indeed. Humility requires us to appreciate what (and Who) we have.

Occasionally, on our DiscipleTrip journey, we will have opportunities to use our finances to bless those around us. A spirit of generosity is a wonderful show of the love of Christ. Consider Peter and John, in Acts, as they approached the crippled beggar at the temple gate. The beggar was asking for money as they walked past him. Then Peter said,

"SILVER OR GOLD I DO NOT HAVE, BUT WHAT I DO HAVE I GIVE YOU. IN THE NAME OF JESUS CHRIST OF NAZARETH, WALK." (ACTS 3:6 NIV)

What they gave him, empowered by the Holy Spirit, was the one thing no money could purchase; his health and his freedom. The money we spend investing in others won't compare, at all, to the Spirit within us, as long as we belong to Him. While considering finances is important, we need to be more concerned with the heart behind our generosity. See abundance in Him, not in your resources.

Chapter 5: Packing for the Trip

"God has gone out of the religious business altogether and solved all the world's problems without anyone needing to perform a single religious duty." – Russ Johnson

WHEN I LEFT COLLEGE, I loaded everything I owned out of the house where I was staying onto a king-sized leopard-print comforter (it was cheap, OK?!) and threw it into the back of my single-cab Ford F-150. I was 23 years old, and I didn't have a clue what I was getting into. All I knew was that God had opened a door and called me to step through it. I had recently graduated from the Arkansas State University College of Business. Through a series of sovereign events, God was leading me to trust Him, by faith, to move a couple of hundred miles away from everything I knew, to share His good news with teenagers, in a city that I knew nothing about.

When I called my fiancée to share the news, she began to cry over the phone. She was confident, and rightfully so, that I was making an unwise decision. By all intents and purposes, my decision-making logic seemed unwise, at best, to anyone other than myself. However, I knew I had heard direction from the Lord on what I was supposed to do.

That first month, I lived in a borrowed house, ate mostly ramen noodles, hot dogs, and mac 'n cheese, and watched, as 35 young men and women made decisions to follow Jesus as their Savior. That particular city in South Arkansas continues to be transformed by the grace of Jesus to this day. The church where I served remains a lighthouse for those who are searching for purpose and direction. I might not have been thriving there by any material means, but spiritually, it felt like I was climbing mountains. Looking back, I realize that the most critical things that I packed were my faith and my willingness. The leopard-print comforter – not so much.

WHAT NOT TO PACK

Knowing what *not* to pack is as important as knowing what *to* pack on your DiscipleTrip. Jesus was very clear as He sent His followers out. He instructed His students to pack light. I believe Jesus was bent on keeping their eyes fixed on the mission rather than getting bogged down with the details along the way. He sent His disciples out, two by two, with the instructions to go into a city and search for a person of peace, and to communicate the Good News of the coming kingdom. Check out the story in Luke 10:

AFTER THIS THE LORD APPOINTED SEVENTY-TWO OTHERS AND SENT THEM ON AHEAD OF HIM, TWO BY TWO, INTO EVERY TOWN AND PLACE WHERE HE HIMSELF WAS ABOUT TO GO. AND HE SAID TO THEM, "THE HARVEST IS

PLENTIFUL, BUT THE LABORERS ARE FEW. THEREFORE, PRAY EARNESTLY TO THE LORD OF THE HARVEST TO SEND OUT LABORERS INTO HIS HARVEST. GO YOUR WAY; BEHOLD, I AM SENDING YOU OUT AS LAMBS IN THE MIDST OF WOLVES. CARRY NO MONEYBAG, NO KNAPSACK, NO SANDALS, AND GREET NO ONE ON THE ROAD. WHATEVER HOUSE YOU ENTER, FIRST SAY, 'PEACE BE TO THIS HOUSE!' AND IF A SON OF PEACE IS THERE, YOUR PEACE WILL REST UPON HIM. BUT IF NOT, IT WILL RETURN TO YOU. AND REMAIN IN THE SAME HOUSE, EATING AND DRINKING WHAT THEY PROVIDE, FOR THE LABORER DESERVES HIS WAGES. DO NOT GO FROM HOUSE TO HOUSE. WHENEVER YOU ENTER A TOWN AND THEY RECEIVE YOU, EAT WHAT IS SET BEFORE YOU. HEAL THE SICK IN IT AND SAY TO THEM, 'THE KINGDOM OF GOD HAS COME NEAR TO YOU.' BUT WHENEVER YOU ENTER A TOWN AND THEY DO NOT RECEIVE YOU, GO INTO ITS STREETS AND SAY, 'EVEN THE DUST OF YOUR TOWN THAT CLINGS TO OUR FEET WE WIPE OFF AGAINST YOU. NEVERTHELESS KNOW THIS, THAT THE KINGDOM OF GOD HAS COME NEAR. (LUKE 10: 1-11)

No money? No sleeping bag? No flip flops?

What was this? Some kind of new reality show where contestants see who can last the longest without basic necessities? Was Jesus simply being cruel?

No, this was not an act of cruelty, but a lesson in divine provision. Jesus was teaching His followers that He would provide for all of their needs, and that they could trust His instructions.

In the last chapter, we discussed counting the cost. Is this chapter in Luke contradicting that message? It could be perceived as such, if you think that the emphasis is on the *material things* we are or are not supposed to "pack." But again, this is where our thinking shifts, once more, from the temporal to the eternal.

The divine lesson is to look, truthfully, at our own situation, pray and ask our Divine Trip Planner what exactly we are to bring, and then follow those instructions to the T. In order to live as God intended for His children to live, we must learn to discern the voice of God. This is not an easy task. Hearing from the Lord is a learned skill that involves spending time together with our Father through prayer and the reading of His Word. This time is critical to experiencing an abundant life in Christ. Be sure you are correctly hearing from Him. (*Discerning the Voice of God*[2] is a terrific book if you want to grow more in this area.) So, if He tells us not to pack a snack, a bag, or even money, we need to follow those instructions exactly – not partially – and we can rest assured that we will see a mighty interaction take place. The point is to understand that, if we have been called, we will indeed be equipped. He's already planned the entire road ahead and He knows what extra baggage will only slow us down. We cannot trust our feelings on this, we can only trust His instruction. Following His direction is always worth it.

Because He's God, He also knows the people that will be used to waylay the mission and slow us down. Remember that verse in Luke 10:4?

Did Jesus just say, don't even say "hi" to those we meet on the road? Doesn't that sound like the opposite of "love your neighbor as yourself" (Mark 12:31)? The key in understanding is to recognize the layers of priority in this instruction.

I think our Savior knew that if the disciples struck up these types of conversations with bystanders, they would be tempted to negotiate or beg for their needs to be met. He did not want them to seek out, from others, what He

---

[2] Discerning the Voice of God: How to Recognize When He Speaks, Priscilla Shirer. Moody Publishers, Chicago 2012.

had already promised to provide. Jesus had bigger plans for His children than to simply feed, water, and clothe them. He wants His followers, us, to learn to trust Him. We are to engage with others for His purpose only – never for our own.

What not to pack? Anything He tells you to leave at home.

What Else to Leave at Home

Ok, so Jesus is writing our packing list. It might mean for us to, literally, take no money, no sleeping bag, and to leave the flip flops. But, most importantly, we'll go by His direction. There are also a couple other things that we simply won't have room for on the trip; other things we have to leave behind. These are the things that won't take up space in the suitcase, but certainly will slow us down in weight. One of those critical items that we will be leaving behind is "ministry," or at least our mainstream ideas about it. Surprised? Consider this dialogue between two guys I knew:

> John: *So, what are you wanting to do with your life?*
>
> Chris: *Man, I really believe God wants me to do ministry.*
>
> John: *Cool, what does that mean?*
>
> Chris: *You know, like, work at a church.*
>
> John: *Gotcha. Hey, you do know that's not necessarily the only way to do ministry, right?*
>
> Chris: *I'm not sure I'm following you.*
>
> John: *Ministry is simply listening to Jesus and doing what He says. It's taking what you have been given and utilizing it for the glory of God. For example, many of the guys I know that are doing the most ministry are guys who work at banks, electrical companies and in coaching roles. What if, instead of looking to get a job in a church, you got in a job utilizing your gifting and used that platform as an opportunity to*

make disciples?

Chris: *You know, I've haven't really thought about it that way. I'm going to seriously consider it.*

Consider this. Ministry is not something you do, it's something you leave behind as a result of following Jesus.

This was a major paradigm shift in my own life. In fact, it took much of the pressure off my shoulders. Much time and energy is wasted in conjuring up good strategies on how to reach people with the Good News of Jesus. Don't get me wrong, there is nothing wrong with planning or even executing formal outreach ministries. When it's all said and done, I'm afraid there will have been more said than done, though. However, there is much power in listening for Jesus' direction and obeying.

When we employ this Spirit-led submission, we open the door for the supernatural. We could spend an entire year formulating an evangelism ministry, recruiting participants, and training our team, with little results. Conversely, you could incorporate this obedience-based ministry by asking your waiter or waitress if there is anything for which you could pray for them before your next meal, if the Spirit prompts. No planning, no committees, no document preparation involved. Just spontaneous, real-life, real-world conversation. That's true ministry.

The call to "full-time ministry" is actually the call of all believers. As John mentioned, it is not about a vocation. It is about a full-time, full-heart commitment. No matter where you are or what job you do, if you are a believer, you should consider it and act accordingly – because you are, indeed, in full-time ministry.

Robert E. Coleman references this in his wonderful book, *The Master Plan for Evangelism*[3]. Paraphrasing Coleman, we get so caught up in creating these massive plans, that we don't realize that the Master's plan was just to stay close to those He was discipling. He stayed with them and they did life together. They didn't have a lot of structured anything. They ate together, they prayed together, they fished together, they traveled together, and they weren't trying to look like they were on mission. They didn't have matching t-shirts. If anything, as ragged as they were, they probably looked like they were on anything but mission! The classroom was the natural landscape, and the greatest teaching opportunities showed up not through a text-book, but through the application of The Book in real life.

So, leave behind your previous idea of "ministry." A DiscipleTrip is not, at all, confined to a small portion of time.

So, What Type of Equipment Are We Actually Packing? What Does it Really Mean to Equip the Saints? Wait, We're Saints?

In Ephesians 4:12-14, Paul tells those who lead the church at Ephesus that their primary job is to:

"EQUIP THE SAINTS FOR THE WORK OF THE MINISTRY, FOR BUILDING UP THE BODY OF CHRIST, UNTIL WE ATTAIN TO THE UNITY OF THE FAITH AND OF THE KNOWLEDGE OF THE SON OF GOD, TO MATURE MANHOOD, TO THE MEASURE

---

[3] The Master Plan of Evangelism, Robert Coleman. Revell, Grand Rapids, MI 2010

OF THE STATURE OF THE FULLNESS OF CHRIST, SO THAT WE MAY NO LONGER
BE CHILDREN, TOSSED TO AND FRO BY THE WAVES…" (ESV)

When the apostle used the word "equip," his audience would have had three word-pictures come to mind. The first meaning of the word would have entailed a soldier being prepared – or "equipped" – for battle.

What does a soldier need in preparation for war? Well, he or she needs a lot of training. The soldier must know how to use the weapon, assure proper hydration and nutrition, follow the commands of a leader, work with his or her team, coordinate a mobile living station, and many other life-saving skills and habits that are required to persevere amidst the harshest of environments. To be equipped as a follower of Christ requires many of the same attributes; but in the spiritual realm. We must learn to develop a healthy Christo-centric worldview, as well as learn to practice the spiritual disciplines and growth habits required to survive in a world that was never intended to be our home.

The second meaning of the word "equip" would have been a medical term that was used to realign a bone or joint that had become misaligned, due to overuse or an injury. Much in the same way, sin has caused our lives to shift out of alignment with God's design for our lives. Our journey back to life includes healing and restoration in and through Christ. He cares about our brokenness and desires to realign our lives with His. He has a beautiful plan for our lives. Ephesians 2:10 tells us that we are God's masterpiece, created in Christ Jesus for good works. When we step into that space, our lives come back into alignment and we can function properly as the Body that God intended.

The third meaning of the word "equip" is to pack a ship for a long journey. I have not been involved in a sailing excursion – although it is on my bucket list –

but I have been on a couple of long journeys into the mountains for extended camping trips. It is crucial that you pack the necessary items in preparation for what might come your way. For example, every serious hiker/camper needs a climbing rope. This rope could be the very piece of equipment that saves your life given certain circumstances. You also need a fire starter for cold evenings and food preparation. You need to pack the appropriate attire for various weather conditions, food that can be consumed on the go, and plenty of water.

To be equipped for the journey of following Jesus, there are also necessary items. God has provided a book, His Holy Bible, that operates as a trail guide for our journey. Within its pages, we read stories of faith, forgiveness, and love. We learn how to treat others, be in relationship with our spouse, and raise healthy children. We find instruction as to how to handle our finances, manage anger, and be generous with what God has given us.

If you, my friend, are a follower of Jesus, then you are a "saint" as this verse references. Whether or not you got out of bed this morning, looked in the mirror, and considered yourself a saint is irrelevant. In Christ, you are being made holy, blameless, and righteous and will be fully completed as such, in His presence in Heaven. You are an image bearer of the Most High, and you need to be equipped for the work of the ministry. As you think through what to pack in your suitcase, sort back through the three descriptions of the word "equip" above, and listen as the Father instructs you on what you may need to bring on this journey.

THE OTHER SUITCASE

Did you know that the enemy is also packing for your trip? Without giving him more credit than he is due – after all he is not omniscient, nor is he omnipresent

– he is active in planning and scheming… and packing. And you can be sure if you are to set out with a heart right for God, that he'll be right behind, trying to trip you up every step of the way. The other suitcase, packed by the enemy of your soul, is already filled to the brim with a customized plan to distract, tempt and harm you, by many means. So, next, we'll talk about how our proper equipment disarms his.

THE NON-NEGOTIABLES, YOUR CARRY-ON

Just like you wouldn't proceed on a long trip without the charger for your phone or the gas in your car, there are two things that are imperative to include on your DiscipleTrip: The Bible and your armor (Eph 6:11). These are your carry-ons. The items that should not be checked and that, no matter what (delay, layover, detour), they shouldn't leave your side.

There are some amazing books out there on the subject of Spiritual Warfare and if you've never read one, I highly suggest considering *Reclaiming Surrendered Ground* [4] and *The Essential Guide to Spiritual Warfare* [5]. The critical thing we need to understand is that God has this trip planned out, and as a result, the enemy is also busy desperately trying to formulate a plan to ensure that we are not successful in realizing God's perfect design for it. His baggage is so packed that it's sure to be one of those that you'd pay extra for on a flight because it's over the weight limit. Everything he wants to sell to you will indeed cost you much, much more than you realize. Anything Satan has to offer you is over-the-limit of what is good for you, in God's eyes. That would be easy to spot if he were, indeed, just carrying around some big bursting-at-the-seams backpack, but that's

---

[4] *Reclaiming Surrendered Ground*, Jim Logan. Moody Publishers Chicago, IL 1995.
[5] *The Essential Guide to Spiritual Warfare*, Neil T. Andersson & Timothy M. Warner. Bethany House, Bloomington, MN 2016

not how he does it; he is good at disguise. In fact, he may look like the "lightest" person or thing on this trip (2 Cor 11:14). This, my friend, is the reality and difficulty of spiritual warfare.

Satan, our enemy, does not appreciate the kingdom initiative that you are taking. In fact, such effort will, undoubtedly, be met with opposition. Yet, we will be equipped to handle it if we pack the correct armor and rely on the Spirit. See, the great news is that even though the enemy has actually got a bag of tricks waiting for us, not one of those items in his bag is new. He's been recycling them since the time of his creation, and he, himself, has no ability to create. His baggage consists of the same things he's had in it from the very beginning – the tricks to lie, kill, and destroy. He may have polished them up to look more like things you are attracted to, but they are still the very same tricks.

However, God has given us the exact list of what to pack; the non-negotiables needed to stand firm and not have our trip waylaid by his schemes (Eph 6:14 - 17). Here's your packing list:

1. The belt of truth.
2. The breastplate of righteousness.
3. The helmet of salvation.
4. The shield of faith.
5. The sword of the Spirit.
6. The shoes of readiness.

In order to be fully prepared for this trip, pay careful attention to each of the pieces of armor, listed above. These are not items that will just sit in your suitcase. Each piece serves a specific purpose and will be used, regularly, on our trip. Let me explain to you how I pack them and how I put them on.

Packing in Prayer

In 1 Thessalonians 5:17, the apostle Paul tells followers of Jesus to pray without ceasing. Paul is not instructing us to fold our hands, close our eyes, and bow our heads for each of the 16, or so, waking hours of the day. Rather, the apostle is teaching his listeners and readers to adopt a lifestyle of communication with their Heavenly Father. Since God is the Alpha and Omega, the beginning and the end, I like to begin each day, before my eyes open, with three requests.

The first thing I do is to pray for the armor of God, piece by piece. Praying for the helmet of salvation helps to remind me to have a sanctified mind, as one who has been transformed by Jesus, thinking on things above rather than things of the Earth.

The breastplate of righteousness protects the heart. In this request, I am reminded that Jesus has given me a new heart that beats with passion and purpose.

The belt of truth reminds me to dismiss any false scripts that I may be believing about myself. It also serves to protect me from any lie that the enemy may be attempting to convince me of, in regard to someone else or even my God.

My feet are shod with the Gospel of Peace and this armor reminds me that Jesus has promised to go with me and even make provision for my steps. Because of the peace of God, I don't have to worry about what today may hold.

The shield of faith protects me from the fiery arrows that Satan may hurl my way. My faith becomes my defense in times of weakness.

Lastly, the sword of the Spirit is my offensive weapon to wield in the battle of everyday life. I have the Spirit of the living God inside of me and can therefore face any obstacle or foe that may come my way.

The second component of my morning prayer includes a request for the filling of the Holy Spirit. I have found that most people struggle to understand and know this third member of the Godhead. Unfortunately, the Holy Spirit seems to be cast as either a sort of mystical, abstract, and unpredictable force or, on the other extreme, a dated and dismissed relic of the early church. However, the Holy Spirit is absolutely necessary for today's believer. He is a guide and a light to our path. He was promised by Jesus before His ascent into Heaven and is described as our *advocate*. We should ask for the presence of the Holy Spirit each day and learn to listen and sense His leadership in our everyday lives.

The third request each morning is for the fruits of the spirit. Relying on our own strength, the virtues of peace, patience, gentleness, self-control, meekness, and long suffering are short lived. But with the Spirit, these fruits are readily available for the child of God. Galatians 5:22 confirms the believer's access to display these virtues through the power of God's Holy Spirit. Simply put, we need to tap into the strength of our Heavenly Father in order to manifest the gifts that we desire to exhibit in our lives.

I enjoy ending each day by thanking God for His provision for that particular day, often listing out any particular moments throughout the day where God seemed to guide and direct my life. In between these morning and evening prayers, we must learn to cast all of our anxieties on Him, because He cares for us (1 Peter 5:7). God can do more in five minutes of prayer than we can do in five years of work. Our Lord sympathizes with our weaknesses and cares for His children. Developing this lifestyle of communication with our Father sets up the believer to walk in step with the creator of the universe as he or she discovers a full and abundant life through the power of Christ.

ANYTHING ELSE?

My prayer for you, my brother or sister, is that you have packed well and are equipped for the journey ahead. If you've got those items, your Bible and your armor, you're geared up. Other than this, as we said before, pray to understand what, if anything else, God wants you to bring and what you would do well to leave home.

It has been my experience that when I listen to the Spirit's prompting, even in the small, seemingly harmless decisions, I reap the rewards. Think that sounds cliché? Consider the two examples below and let's wrap this up on a humorous note.

In preparing for a visit to my accountant, one year, to complete my tax return, I held a folder in my hand, at home, of personal insurance documents and considered whether to bring it. I had a "feeling," which I later believed was a prompting, to bring the folder, but I talked myself out of it. I believed I had all the pertinent information I'd need and didn't want to carry "extra baggage." Yes, we love the irony, especially considering it was a small folder. As I'm sure you've already deduced, my insurance agent asked for this very document that I had left at home, and, as a result, had to wait to proceed on the processing of my paperwork until this information was obtained. Still, thinking it was no big deal, I got home and promptly prepared to scan and email it over. It wouldn't have been an issue of course, assuming my scanner decided to work, as normal, and my computer wasn't having problems. And then the Wi-Fi went out, so I couldn't send anything. Hilarious. What could have taken three seconds of my time to open the folder and hand the document over, took two hours of time to work through the technical difficulties to get it there, and, of course, a lot of unnecessary aggravation. And, naturally, all of it also delayed my refund. Could you believe God cares and pays attention to things as little as a single document in our lives? You bet He does.

Our next example is slightly bigger than a piece of paper, though.

I was rushing out the door one day to get to an appointment. Truthfully, I was going to Bible Study with my regular Friday group. I was just barely on time and was hustling, as I left the house and locked the door. Pulling off my driveway, I realized I had accidently flipped on the outside light by the front door when I left. Since it was the middle of the day, there was no reason for the light to stay on and waste electricity for the next few hours. But of course, since I was already on a tight schedule, I contemplated for a second just leaving it on and getting it when I came back. I actually went back in forth in my mind, twice, and couldn't figure out why I had the feeling to just "leave it be," when it clearly wasn't good stewardship of our electric bill to leave it on. Again, great irony – spoiler alert.

I quickly pulled back up the driveway, threw the car into "park," or at least I believed I did, and jumped out of the car to unlock the front door, flip off the switch and CRRRRRRAAAAAAAASSSSSSHHHH.

The gear slipped – yes, likely from user error and being rushed – and instead of staying in park, the car slid forward and drove through the garage door. For real. $800 later, and a breath-holding call to my spouse, during work, to explain that I had driven through the garage. Needless to say, I didn't make it Bible study that day either.

Hopefully, you've had a good laugh with me.

Seriously though, consult the Spirit. The Word says He reveals all truth (John 16:13) and because God pays attention to even the slightest details (Heb 4:13), He will guide you in the "seemingly" little decisions, like what to pack and how to park. Learn from my examples, that it's not always as "little" as you think.

Chapter 6: Our Trip Mates

"There is simply no substitute for getting with people, and it is ridiculous to imagine that anything less, short of a miracle, can develop strong Christian leadership." - Robert Coleman, The Master Plan of Evangelism

WHEN I FIRST FELT COMPELLED to disciple-making, through the prompting of the Holy Spirit, I invited Nolan on the journey. Nolan was an adventure-loving guy, who was always up for a good time and was a joy to be around. We immediately connected in friendship and I decided that I would begin investing in him, spiritually. After our second time hanging out, we had discussed camping gear, future adventure plans, and even considered a joint business venture. However, it was clear to see that he had little or no desire to move forward in a spiritual journey of any sort. In hindsight, I realize that I was very unclear as to my intentions with our time together and I could have done more to lay the foundation for a Jesus-centered relationship. I guess I had taken for granted that it might come along with the friendship that developed, but, when he moved, I realized the opportunity that had been largely lost.

In contrast, I want to tell you about a friend of mine, named Randy. Randy has a checkered past. His story is full of brokenness, in many areas of his life. Randy came to know the love of Jesus after a life-long struggle with addiction. His choices led him to his last resort. Renewal Ranch is a local ministry that specializes in helping men discover a life free from addiction, through a relationship with Christ. At the time of this writing, Randy is in his fifth year of recovery and has experienced a dramatic change from the life he once lived. In the last couple years of our DiscipleTrip, Randy has procured a job that he loves, regained the family that he almost lost, moved into my neighborhood and is now involved in a seminary-level Bible study, geared at helping him take others on a journey with Jesus. Randy recently sat down with me over coffee and spent a half hour teaching me what Jesus is teaching him regarding living a faith-filled life.

God has used both of these men in my life to teach me different aspects of those along the road. And with that, I'm realizing how critical it is for us to keep company.

WHY WE CAN'T GO IT ALONE

Have you ever looked at the shape of the cross? God does nothing by accident. The cross provides us with the visual image of the two most important commandments, according to Jesus (Luke 10:27-28, Matt 22:37-40, Mark 12:30-31); to love God and to love your neighbor. The love for God should be above and significantly more extended than any other love in your life (Luke 14:26). Notice that the vertical piece on the cross is the longer one, and it provides the stability for the smaller, horizontal piece. The vertical piece represents our direct relationship with God.

The horizontal piece represents our love extended towards others. While critically important, it cannot be in place without the vertical piece holding it there.

And if we take this a step further, we can see when Jesus was crucified, His hands were outstretched on the horizontal piece. His heart sank further down, as his body did, and hung nearest to the vertical piece. Jesus' heart, soul, and spirit were with God (Luke 23:46), but His hands were outstretched to us.

The cross is the visual representation of, not only how much God loves us (John 3:16), but also how we are supposed to live, as Christians. We cannot ignore the horizonal part of our relationship with Christ.

So Where Do They Come From? Finding People Along the Way

Let me tell you about one of my trip mates and how his journey relates to the tires of transformation. I met Paul on the baseball field. In fact, I was coaching his son that season. While we were standing on the baseball diamond making small talk, I asked him if he had plans for the weekend.

Paul: *"Yeah, I'm throwing a private concert featuring RUN DMC for my top salesmen at Hewlett-Packard."* The air quickly escaped my lungs.

Me: *"Cool, …uh, I plan on hanging around the house."*

Paul: *"You wanna come?"*

Me: *"Heck yeah!"*

And that's how I got to know Paul. That's also the weekend that I peed in the stall next to RUN DMC, The Godfather of ol' school hip hop. He signed my Adidas cap, that night, and Paul and I started a friendship that lasts to this day.

When Paul started his journey, he wasn't a follower of Christ. He had attended a couple of different churches, but ultimately walked out after a memorable event occurred at the childhood church where his family attended, following the tragic events of September 11, 2001. That particular Sunday, the preacher announced that he believed the best thing for America to do would be to fly over the Middle East and bomb all of those terrorists so that they could get what was coming to them. Being of Middle Eastern decent, the entire Ayoub family walked out of that church building, never to return.

So, it was understandable when Paul told me that, while he thought it was cool that I had planted a church, he wasn't "all that religious." He said his goal in life was to work hard and support his family; two traits that I admire in him still today.

After a few baseball games that first season, we invited Paul and his wonderful wife Catie over to our house for dinner. We had the best time laughing and telling stories while our kids played together. On their way out, Paul told me that was the first time they could remember eating dinner in a friend's house since college.

Three years later, Paul is the most hospitable person I know. He and his wife intentionally invite one family over, each week, and prepare and meal to share together. Their house is a place where I feel safe and loved, as much as in my own home. Paul is now leading a monthly men's lunch geared at sharing burgers and helping other men, not only become disciples of Jesus, but also engage in disciple-making efforts in the lives of others. Paul has moved through the Tires of Transformation (more on this later in the chapter), from a man who was spiritually dead to an infant in the faith, and, now, past a young adult and into a spiritual parent. I have watched as God has radically transformed his life in three short years.

Just last year, Paul's father passed away. I sat on the other end of the phone as he walked his own extended family through the grieving process and pointed them to his faith in Jesus as a foundation for life. He honored his father at his funeral and has counseled his own mother and other relatives in their own lives. Paul would say that our time together has been a huge blessing to him and his family. However, I am convinced that the blessing of watching Paul's transformation has impacted me as much, if not more so, than it has impacted him.

Keep an open eye out for Trip Mates to join you in your metaphorical journey through disciple-making in the everyday rhythms of your life. The blessing of watching God do His work, and the privilege of being used by Him, is one that will never be forgotten and forms relationships that can never be broken. It is often in the journey with Jesus that we realize how much we enjoy others and their importance within our own journey.

As you move forward in your DiscipleTrip, you will begin to see the world around you come to life. In fact, it is impossible to spend time with Jesus in the company of others without beginning to notice those that you encounter along the way. A growing love for others has always been an identifying mark of those who are growing in Christ. The more time we spend with Jesus, the more we are captivated by His love. And the more we are moved by His love, the more we begin to notice the people around us. We will notice strangers and even find ourselves curious as to the circumstances in their lives. It's almost as if the love that we feel from Jesus begins to spill over into the lives of those that we come in contact with. In fact, one of Jesus' more famous sayings is "they (others) will know that you are my followers by the way that you love one another" (John 13:35). To love in a vertical relationship with the Savior is to love those around us horizontally. As we go, we grow.

But Who, Really, is My Neighbor?

...AND "WHO IS MY NEIGHBOR?" FOR HE WAS TESTING THE MESSIAH.
(LUKE 10:29)

This question came on the heels of a test posed by a lawyer to the Son of God. You see, the lawyer was searching for something. He knew there had to be more to life than the religious systems that he was engaged in. He wanted to know what Jesus would say was the key to eternal life. But Jesus answered his question with a question. He asked the man what he had read in the Law – this was the name of a section in the Jewish "Bible" before the life and teaching of Jesus were recorded. The man answered correctly, noting the whole summation of the law, "You shall love the Lord your God with all your heart and with all your soul and with all your strength and with all your mind, and your neighbor as yourself." Then Jesus said to him, "You have answered correctly; do this, and you will live."

Next, Jesus shares the parable of the Good Samaritan. The beauty of this story lies in the compassion that a complete stranger had for one who was broken down and hurting on the side of the road. However, Jesus was talking to a religious audience and sharing about a religious man who was too busy to care for those around him. His story was not only an indictment to the lives that the religious professionals were living, but also imagery showing how much compassion that He would show broken men and women like themselves.

So, as we travel along the road of life, trusting Jesus in the company of friends, we grow in love. We grow in compassion for those along the way. And as we journey together, we see the love and grace of Jesus working through our lives and into the lives of those we come in contact with.

BUT YOU STILL HAVEN'T ANSWERED MY QUESTION

Who does God want us to invite on this transformative trip? Who might God be wanting to change with us as we stay in close proximity to Him? The short answer is, drumroll please… I don't know. But here's what I do know. He already knows. This is the point in the adventure where we push pause and pray.

No, really. Stop reading and pray.

Seriously.

As you pray, ask the Father who He would like for us to bring into this DiscipleTrip; into this relationship. And then listen. Really listen.

Maybe God has already put a person on your mind or placed them deep in your heart. Maybe God has placed that person right next to you in your office, or at the same table with you in your home. But maybe He hasn't… yet. Let me encourage you to be patient. He will bring the exact person, or people, into your life at exactly the right time. Maybe that person is not quite ready to make the trip with you just yet. Or maybe you are not ready to journey with them. Either way, don't be afraid of the wait. It is in this place that God wants to work. When it is time for you to know who He wants you to take on this DiscipleTrip journey with you, you will know, and not a minute too soon. And we may not have to look far at all.

Until He makes that clear, let me stir your thinking with some things I've learned.

HOW TO KNOW

The number one criterion for a Trip Mate is a willingness to travel. Now, I don't mean someone who wants to see the world at the drop of a hat. I am speaking figuratively. Consider what Robert Coleman pointed out in *The Master Plan of Evangelism* summarizing that "men were His method:"

> *"His concern was not with programs to reach the multitudes,
> but with men whom the multitudes would follow."*

Jesus's concern was in finding willing and teachable men who would naturally inspire others to do the same. Nothing else in their qualifications mattered as much as the interest of their hearts, even despite their outward filth. In talking about the very men Jesus chose for His first DiscipleTrip, Coleman continues:

> *"By any standard of sophisticated culture then and now they would surely be
> considered as a rather ragged collection of souls. One might wonder how Jesus could
> ever use them. They were impulsive, temperamental, easily offended, and had all the
> prejudices of their environment… They were indeed 'unlearned and ignorant'
> according to the world's standard (Acts 4:13), but they were teachable."*

These ragged, but "teachable," men were the same men that Jesus confirmed would have a seat at His table and sit on the thrones judging the twelve tribes of Israel (Luke 22:28-20). We cannot underestimate the importance of a willing traveler; it's imperative.

WHAT ABOUT NON-BELIEVERS?

Remember when we talked about our departure point? Well on the most amazing DiscipleTrip ever, the guys on the trip had no idea they were about to even embark on a trip, ahead of time. They were busy going about their daily life at work when they were summoned, unexpectedly. There was no job application, ministry meeting, or talent that qualified them for the journey. In fact, many of those that were encountered on this first DiscipleTrip were not initially believers. But they were still willing to go. And it's in the presence of Jesus that they were, undeniably, changed.

Because the Word confirms that "every knee shall bow at the name of Jesus" (Rom 14:11), non-believers simply cannot remain unmoved by the Word of God and His Spirit. They will either retreat in disgust (2 Cor 2:16), consider it crazy or "foolish" (1 Cor 2:14), or will be so deeply cut by its sword that serious healing will need to be administered. While we cannot control anyone's actions, other than our own, we can, with God's help, recognize the need to be available for emergent Holy Spirit care.

So, can a non-believer accompany us on a DiscipleTrip? Absolutely. As we said before, the criteria for a DiscipleTrip is not belief, it is the willingness to go. Willingness is the movement that sets the wheel in motion.

In short, it doesn't matter where your Trip Mates begin their journey. In fact, it doesn't matter where you begin your journey. The important part is that you start. In order to help you understand where you are beginning your journey and where we are going from here, I want to introduce you to a diagram that we are calling the "Tires of Transformation."

THE TIRES OF TRANSFORMATION

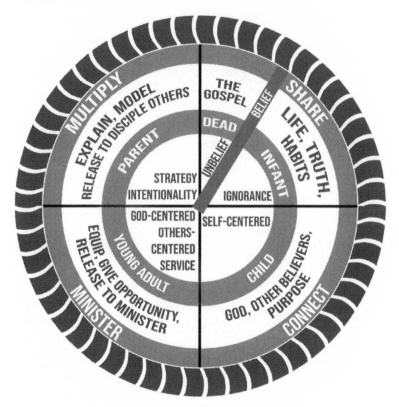

As you begin to familiarize yourself with this tool, I want to give a shout out to Jim Putnam of Real-Life Ministries for the inspiration behind this diagram; one he called the Wheel of Spiritual Maturity. While I've added onto his original concept, the inspiration of Jim's work has revolutionized the way I think about discipleship and I believe it will greatly change the way you view, not only being a disciple of Jesus, but making disciples, as well.

As you can see from the tire, there are many different levels of spiritual maturity. In fact, these transformation levels are accurately comparative to the stages of development in any human being. Before we are infants, we are unborn. In this same way, we are dead in our sin before we know Christ. If we receive the Gospel of Jesus, we move into the infant stage of our journey. In this stage, we are incredibly vulnerable. We are easily tossed by the waves of life, doctrine, and understanding. We must learn basic spiritual truths, be exposed to real life examples of life change, and be hungry to grow and learn about the life that we have been given in Christ.

After the infancy stage, we grow up to be children in the faith. As children, we are self-centered in our new nature and have the tendency to believe that our faith is ultimately about our happiness, our growth, or even our personal fulfillment. It is in this stage, that we desperately need connection to other believers, God – through development of spiritual disciplines, and scripture. As we grow to become self-feeders, who rely on God for our daily provision, we begin to transform into young adults in the faith. Just like adults in their teens and twenties, and even into our thirties, we can become convinced that we know all there is to know about everything. In this stage, we can become cynical of others, suspect to those in authority over us, and even theorists rather than partakers in the kingdom. Young adults need equipping. They need someone who is further in the transformation process to walk with them, rather than to shame them. Young adults need to get in the game. They need opportunities to serve and connect to the mission and purposes of God in our world.

Once young adults get the experience of using their gifts for a higher purpose, they begin to move into the parenting stage of transformation. It is in this stage that the person realizes not only God's command to make disciples, but also engages in that process. Parents need opportunities, not only to make disciples who make disciples, but also to be able to describe the process in a way that is reproducible for others.

It is my hope that the Tire of Transformation helps you to see that anyone is a candidate to embark on a DiscipleTrip. Whether they are a believer or not yet a believer, recently a convert or a seasoned Christian, everyone has the ability to move forward in the journey. In fact, the parent stage of transformation is simply the beginning phase for sharing the Good News of Jesus and repeating the entire process. The tires should never stop turning. If we feel that we, or anyone else, has arrived, then we are simply hung up on one phase of the transformation and need to be reengaged in the turning of the tire.

Most people envision discipleship as a post-conversion process. However, I would like to challenge that notion. I believe that this entire tire represents the discipleship process. It is not that 3/4 of the tire represents the process and the other 1/4 represents evangelism. It is all within the process of making disciples. The sharing of the good news of Jesus' death, burial, and resurrection is a natural outflow of the life of a mature disciple of Christ.

We also must accept that we cannot move someone along in the journey, only the Holy Spirit can do that. We cannot move someone from death into life either, that is also the job of the Holy Spirit. We cannot judge who is worthy to receive the words of Jesus that we share or even who seems to be progressing in the faith. We'd be overstepping our bounds, to do so. Do you know who is the only rightful owner of that job? You guessed it; it's the work of the Holy Spirit.

Knowing this, discipleship can be demystified. Discipleship is simply us staying in close proximity with Jesus and with others, as our hearts aim to serve Him. The Spirit does the work and the movement of transformation. He is the one who keeps the tire inflated and moving in the right direction.

Chapter 7: Exit 99 for Route 1

"…at this point if one were to measure the effectiveness of his evangelism by the number of his converts, Jesus doubtless would not be considered among the most productive mass evangelists of the church."
- Robert Coleman, The Master Plan of Evangelism

THERE'S NO QUESTION that many of us are surrounded by a plethora of people that we'd call "friends" over Facebook or other social media sites. Yet there are very few people in this world that become true, life-long friends. Social media is not real community, and it does not represent relationship the way Jesus intended it. Jesus was willing to see more and invest more than we are often willing to do. As we discussed earlier, we don't need to try to reach the world with a platform. But we do need to try to reach whomever is in our world, with a willing heart. And to Jesus, a willing heart is the priceless reflection of He who would have left it all, for even one soul.

In Matthew 18:12, Jesus says, ""What do you think? If a man owns a hundred sheep, and one of them wanders away, will he not leave the ninety-nine on the hills and go to look for the one that wandered off?" One disciple, one believer, one "Trip Mate," just one soul, was important enough to Jesus to temporarily leave the 99 to return the one home. There is much for us to consider, on a DiscipleTrip, of the purpose of "one."

FIRST, THE ONE

As we discussed earlier, there's no point in a DiscipleTrip other than to glorify and follow the commands of The One who gave them, Jesus Christ.

In glorifying our King, we begin to find *our* place in *His* story. We get joy when we get Jesus. Our "follow-ship" of Jesus cannot be separated from the mission that He has given us to "fellow-ship" with others. Don't get me wrong, we all get excited about adventure. As you can tell, I love a good road trip, but there has to be something more. Adventure can't be our motivating force. In my own life, the adventure has a tendency to become the object of my worship, or in other words, the *adventure can easily become an idol.*

The eloquent preacher John Piper once called the human heart an *idol factory.* We pump out idols created out of good things every day. With good intentions at heart, Christians have the innate ability to make idols out of our kids, our hobbies, and our careers. We quickly make our friends our idols. And we can even do the same with our spouses. We are keen at taking good things and converting them into "God things." This is a form of idolatry. No *thing* on this Earth should ever become central to our worship.

If you are seeking to embark on a DiscipleTrip of your own, take caution as you may develop the desire to idolize your good work for King Jesus into something that it was never intended to be. We must *be* before we *do*. We were created in the image of God. We are *human beings* and not *human doings*. We must not become so invested in our work that we forget that it is His work on the cross that brings peace, joy, and fulfillment.

We cannot give what we do not have from a heart impressed upon by the Holy Spirit. In order to guide someone in their own journey with Jesus, you must have first experienced Him yourself. The Gospel is not only good news when it is first received, but it also provides the power to continue in your daily walk.

We must find our hope and joy in Jesus and nothing that this world has to offer, including the adventure.

SECOND, THE ONE

Now that we've established Who the trip is for, it's up to Him to point us to who should be on the journey with us. Yes, we can and maybe should invite many – if that's the prompting of the Holy Spirit. But we shouldn't be surprised or disappointed if an entire DiscipleTrip is just meant to be traveled with one other person. Why? Because a trip for "one" may be much more effective than you initially think.

The brilliance in Jesus' strategy for discipleship is the focus on multiplication and not on addition. He could have easily swayed millions with miracles, even within His short, three-year ministry, and added to the population of believers at a pace nobody would be able to duplicate in the future. Or, He could lead by example, create new examples that were capable of leading and set forth a domino effect of believers creating believers creating believers. The first strategy could have been massive and fast, but potentially short-lived once that generation of believers died. But the second strategy is full of endurance, stability, vitality, and exponential increase.

BCF Ministries (The Biblical Counseling Foundation) highlights an awesome way to understand the power of multiplying a few disciples versus adding many disciples. As they point out, Jesus "concentrated His ministry on only a few disciples with the goal of training them in depth. He trained them so thoroughly that they were then able to repeat His example in reaching others."[6] Now, what if we did the same? What does the math actually look like?

If we discipled just two people per year, focusing our entire year to in-depth discipleship with them to ensure that they'd be able to duplicate the effort with two others, the astounding result shows up in a beautifully significant number of years. By multiplying disciples just two per year, the entire world's population of (currently) 7.5 billion people would be discipled in just 33 years. The human life span of Jesus Christ was also 33 years.

So, in other words, start with the one He brings you. Train up a disciple and then by year two, you and the new disciple take on one new person, each to start the multiplication effect by two.

By comparison, if we were able to simply "add" 100,000 new disciples each day, by year 33, only 1.2 billion would be actually be discipled. Following the addition method would actually take over 180 years to achieve the same number of disciples. Even with our best efforts, the addition doesn't add up.

---

[6] BCF Ministries, Self-Confrontation Bible Study Student Workbook, W18.

By initially focusing on the one, we are, indeed, tending to the masses, in the most effective way possible.

> *"Though he did what he could to help the multitudes, he had to devote himself primarily to a few men, rather than the masses, so that the masses could at last be saved. This was the genius of his strategy."*
> *- Robert Coleman, The Master Plan of Evangelism*

LASTLY, REMEMBER WHEN YOU WERE THE ONE

The Bible is full of Scripture reminding us to remember where we came from. Instead of also wiping our memories of the sin and filth we might have once been caught up in, He gave us the gift of memory so that we could connect and learn to understand the necessity and depth of gratitude justified for His saving grace. While we're not to live (or focus) in the past, we are also not to forget where we came from. It's the most powerful part of our testimony.

My friend, and co-laborer in Christ, runs a local nonprofit that helps take the good news of Jesus into the lives and homes of at-risk teens, through the process of mentoring. Daniel Tyler is a product of the reconciliatory work of Jesus Christ. Once a troubled teen, himself, Daniel witnessed his very own mother pass from this life after being brutally beaten by a boyfriend. Weeks later, Daniel saw the abuser on a bicycle. The man had recently gotten out of prison on bail, and, at that moment, Daniel's instincts kicked in and he sped his SUV to 55 miles per hour. Right before impact, the Spirit of the Lord impressed on Daniel to spare the man's life. He recalls hearing the words, "I died to save your life and I did the same for this man; he just doesn't know it yet." Daniel wept as he drove back to his workplace. Weeks later, he began meeting with the man who was responsible for taking his mother's life, and, by the grace of God, Daniel led the man to the Lord. As Daniel held the hands that claimed the life of his mother, he recalls the emotions of forgiveness that would not have been possible if he hadn't himself, received the same forgiveness from the Lord a decade prior.

At one point, you, too, were the one God chased after; or perhaps, is still after now. Be willing to see others the way He sees them. His creation is precious in His sight.

"A few people so dedicated in time will shake the world for God."
- Robert Coleman, The Master Plan of Evangelism

Chapter 8: How Do We Get There?

"Knowledge was gained by association before it was understood by explanation." - Robert Coleman, The Master Plan of Evangelism

WHEN YOU GO ON A TRIP, you usually type the address into your GPS. A DiscipleTrip has a dynamic address. Ready for it?

DiscipleTrip is CPJ + CPO = MI

Ok, so it's not actually an address, but rather a formula that will work to any destination that you choose. The formula is all about proximity. There are two issues of proximity to ensure transformation on a DiscipleTrip.

The first, and most important concept is to remain in close proximity to Jesus (**CPJ**). The second is to remain in close proximity to others (**CPO**). When we combine the two, living in close proximity to Jesus and in close proximity to others, we can experience maximum impact (**MI**).

If we are going to enter into this closeness, we must first learn to relate. Jesus famously said, "Greater love hath no man than this, that he lay down his life for his friends" (John 15:13). I am convinced that discipleship is relationship. Spending His most valuable resource, His time, with His friends, Jesus knew how to love others.

THE IMPORTANCE OF CPJ & CPO TO PRODUCE MI

Have you ever experienced a white-out?

For as long as our two children have been in school, our Spring Breaks are spent in a town called Pagosa Springs. The ski resort, located on the outskirts of this quaint and southern ski town, boasts of more snowfall, per year, than any other resort in Colorado. It is the time of year that we get most excited about. For the last couple of years, we have loaded down our Honda Pilot with gear, food, and DVDs and left out, sometime around 3 a.m. for the 14.5-hour journey.

Interestingly enough, there are generally 30-60 close friends who make the journey with us. It was on one of these trips that I experienced my first ever white-out. It was a Sunday morning, and I couldn't get to the mountain soon enough. We were some of the first ones in the lift ticket line and the snow was pounding at the base of the resort. Like a kid on Christmas morning, I jumped on the lift, with another brave soul from our hometown, and headed up the mountain. The kids stayed at home on this particular day, because the weather was predicted to be insane. Some 7-9 inches of fresh powder was expected, and, this time, the weather man seemed to predict it with pinpoint accuracy. By the time we got to the top of Alberta Peak at the Wolf Creek Ski Resort, which stands proudly at 11,870 feet in elevation, we were unable to see the trees in the ridge line below us. In fact, you could only see vague outlines at a mere 10-20 feet in distance. I soon discovered that these were some of the most dangerous conditions for snowboarders and that only those with strong riding skills and an expert knowledge of the mountain should be out in such a blizzard. By the grace of God, a couple of guys, who did not exactly fit the criteria, made it down without injury.

There have been many times when I have experienced a sincere lack of clarity in regard to my own life. These are the times when I feel like I am operating in a white-out. As a pastor, I have faced anxiety and even wrestled with seasons of depression. It is in these times, that I am generally relying on my own strength and failing to stay in close proximity to Jesus; finding my true identity and worth in His finished work on the cross.

There are other times when I am walking with my Savior but failing to walk closely with others. These are the times when I live selfishly and am prone to drift toward legalism. That is, I quickly become religious and have a propensity to look down on those that I come in contact with.

But, when I am doing it right, or should I say when I am following directions right, well, that's when the good life happens. Don't confuse the good life that I am referring to with an easy life. You see, there is a large difference in the two. While it is generally not easy, it is worthwhile. These are times when Jesus is guiding me and I get to play a very important role in the lives of others. These are truly the sweetest moments that have Maximum Impact for the kingdom, here on Earth and for all of eternity.

Fellowship is critical to avoiding the white-out. We get "there," by going with others. This is what DiscipleTrip is all about.

Now that you have considered what to bring on your DiscipleTrip, and what not to bring, let's shift our focus toward what we will be doing. In this chapter, I want to give you some extremely practical direction on the "how-to" of DiscipleTrip. I believe it is important to get into some action steps that you can begin to take, immediately, to invite the transformation of the Holy Spirit into your everyday life. It is one thing to talk about taking a DiscipleTrip; it is another thing to actually embark on an adventure. Let's break this concept into multiple categories: First, we will have daily routines. Then, we will look at overall objectives. Lastly, let's consider impromptu and organic opportunities.

DAILY ROUTINE FOR MI

Our daily routine will involve a three-part process. I believe that the following simple, yet effective three practices are not only ancient, but remain incredibly powerful for ushering in the power of Jesus in our current reality.

The first is to pour a cup of coffee. Just kidding! But really, I do find it helps! The real first part of the routine is to interact with the Word of God. Remember our equation?

Close Proximity to Jesus + Close Proximity to Others = Maximum Impact

Interacting with the Word of God positions us closely with Jesus. The Bible is His inspired and written word, and reading the Bible is the key that can unlock even the hardest of hearts. In fact, the Bible even refers to Jesus as The Word (John 1:1).

2 Peter 1:3-4 says:

"HIS DIVINE POWER HAS GRANTED TO US ALL THINGS THAT PERTAIN TO LIFE AND GODLINESS, THROUGH THE KNOWLEDGE OF HIM WHO CALLED US TO HIS OWN GLORY AND EXCELLENCE, BY WHICH HE HAS GRANTED TO US HIS PRECIOUS AND VERY GREAT PROMISES, SO THAT THROUGH THEM YOU MAY BECOME PARTAKERS OF THE DIVINE NATURE, HAVING ESCAPED FROM THE CORRUPTION THAT IS IN THE WORLD BECAUSE OF SINFUL DESIRE."

Did you catch that? *All things* that pertain to life and godliness. What power we've been granted!

In order to access that divine power, we must press into His promises. God's word is a treasure vault that contains infinite pearls and riches, to be discovered by the reader. There have been times in my life where I come across a word, so powerful, in Scripture that it is as if the Lord of the universe is speaking directly into my heart and bringing spiritual direction to current circumstances. Some mornings, I pour an extra cup of coffee for the empty chair next to me, because I know that it is not empty. The king of Glory is *with me*, and an acknowledgement of His presence is the very thing that changes the trajectory of my day. When we read the Word of God, we position ourselves closely to the person and work of Jesus.

Close Proximity to Jesus + **Close Proximity to Others** = Maximum Impact

But don't stop here. Remember, Christianity is a team sport. It is in your best interest to interact with Scripture on a personal level each day, but maximum impact is contingent upon doing so in close proximity to others. Encourage your Trip Mates to read, as well, and then invite them to share in the Word of God together. This invitation to share in the Word of God together is perhaps the most critical routine aspect of a DiscipleTrip.

The second component of a healthy daily routine is to confess sin to one another. This ancient practice brings those on the DiscipleTrip together, around their limitations, before a limitless King. There is power in repentance. Confessing sins is often overlooked, but it is an essential practice for the church of today.

We've gotten away from this practice, as a Body. I am convinced that this lack of transparency castrates the people of God from the power that they were designed to possess. This is the critical component of a DiscipleTrip that forges bonds and creates "Koinonia" for the family of God. Koinonia is the ancient, New Testament word for "fellowship" which implies a level of intimate connection, so deep, that the family is spiritually knit together, in a tightly woven pattern, with colors that are nearly inseparable. As your bond with your Trip Mates grows, so should the level of transparency. I believe one's level of vulnerability, in proximity to others, is proportional to the level of transformation in one's life; so that their life in Christ is not simply talked about, but experienced, firsthand.

The third component of a daily routine, to support MI, is prayer. This should incorporate, not only praying for one another as sin is confessed, but also praying for the lost around you. I personally know "followers of Jesus," today, who cannot name one lost friend. As children to the King, we are called to mimic the mission of Jesus in bringing Good News to those who are lost, hurting, broken, and in desperate need of a Savior. Praying for the lost will open the door to a spiritual journey, as we become attuned to the needs of those we befriend along the journey of our DiscipleTrip. It will also set the foundation for great conversation, as miracles are witnessed in collaboration, instead of in isolation.

OVERALL OBJECTIVES OF MI

Close Proximity to Jesus + Close Proximity to Others = **Maximum Impact**

What is Maximum Impact?

Years ago, a couple of friends and I responded to a Facebook ad geared at prompting folks to apply for a role as an extra in a movie that was going to be shot in Central Arkansas. Our applications were accepted, and the fun began! We were very excited to get to check off an item on our respective bucket lists: to play an extra in a movie! My friends, Carson and Lane, were chosen to be a part of an angry mob of people protesting at the State Capitol building. I was given the role of a cameraman documenting the event at the capitol. We had an absolute blast in filming this scene. I, later, got a call back to shoot a scene involving a community activists' lunch meeting. In this role, I sat at an auxiliary table and enjoyed a breakfast consisting of steak and eggs. The beginning of the shot focused on my hands, as I cut the steak, and then the camera panned from my hands to the table, where the leaders were meeting. My wife also sat in as an extra, at the next table over. I have never eaten so slowly in all my life. The scene took about three hours to shoot and our food ended up cold, but still delicious, by the time we wrapped. The entire experience was memorable. The film was called "God's Not Dead: 2."

The night the movie debuted at our local theatre, we attempted to make, yet another, memory. We called up to the theatre and notified the management that three actors from the recent film would love to make a red-carpet appearance, sign autographs, and meet guests as they came in. The manager was excited and made provisions in the theatre lobby for a meet and greet before the show. So, there we were, three unknowns, pulling up to the theatre in a bright red Mini

Cooper car, complete with red carpet and even a couple of friends with cameras and lanyards labeled "media crew!" After signing autographs and taking pictures in our black tuxedos, with dozens of movie patrons, for a solid half hour, our host walked us into the reserved section of a packed theatre where three empty seats awaited our arrival.

Looking back, the entire experience was ridiculous. We were convinced that we would get boo-ed out of the theatre after the show due to the fact that we were merely extras in the movie, but we, surprisingly, continued to be greeted and photographed on the way out. I'm not even sure anyone knew what scenes we were in, because our appearances are quick and in the background. I suppose the backdrop of this story screams of our culture's fixation with Hollywood. Regardless, reflecting on this activity forces me to consider a spiritual aspect.

I want my life to count for something greater than myself. I would much rather play a small and insignificant role in the background of a story that really mattered, than to "star" in a major production that does nothing for the Kingdom. I want to be a part of something that really moves people – a story worth telling and retelling. I want to have an insignificant role in the story of God. A story that transcends space and time. A story where the hero leaves His place of comfort and lives among everyday people. People who won't know who He is. People who will despise Him. People who will mock Him. And people who will forever be changed by His life and teachings. I want to live my life subscribing to the ultimate Hero's tale. A man who was despised and rejected by men, the only man who ever lived a perfect life but willingly gave His life as a ransom for the very men and women who would deny Him. The Son of God who, through His life, death, burial, and resurrection, conquered evil forever, and will rule and reign throughout all of eternity. I want to live my life for maximum impact. I am convinced that the best way to do that very thing is through the holy work of disciple-making.

When we spend time with Jesus, in close proximity to others, He will do the heavy lifting of eternal transformation; both in us, and in those we walk alongside. This is Maximum Impact.

IMPROMPTU & ORGANIC OPPORTUNITIES TO CREATE MI

Jesus was the King of intentional living. He took many opportunities to stop what He was doing to meet the needs of others. Consider just a few of the stories from His life where seemingly "organic" and "impromptu" opportunities resulted in eternal maximum impact.

In Luke 19:2-3, Jesus was walking through Jericho with a large crowd in tow. It is here that we first meet a man named Zacchaeus. Scripture says that Zacchaeus had two distinguishing characteristics, short in stature and deep in pockets. He seized an opportunity to run ahead of the crowd and climbed a sycamore-fig tree to catch a better glimpse of the Messiah. When the Savior locked eyes with the sinner, Jesus invited Himself to Zacchaeus' home. Although many others muttered at Jesus' house visit to yet another notorious scammer, Jesus was proclaiming Zaccheaus' salvation, as a result of his belief. Verse 10 reinstates the purpose of God's trip to Earth, through the person and work of His Son, Jesus, "For the Son of Man came to seek and to save the lost." The Son of Man did not see this vertically challenged sinner as a distraction, but rather the purpose of His mission.

Jesus also took the time to love children. At one point of Jesus' divine teaching, the people began bringing their own kids to Jesus so that "He might lay hands on them and pray" (Matthew 19:13). The disciples rebuked the people, but Jesus said, "Let the little children come to Me and do not hinder them, for to such belongs the kingdom of Heaven" (14). In this story, Jesus sees these small, habitually undervalued members of the community and adds value to them by giving of His full attention. People were not an inconvenience - even the smallest of them – to the Creator of the universe.

Jesus also showed compassion to the women that He came in contact with. During the time that the Gospels were recorded, women were widely regarded as second-class citizens. In John chapter 4, Jesus not only takes time to show compassion to a woman, but one who was also Samaritan by birth. The Samaritans were known as "half-breeds," the products of Jews who had intermarried with other races of people. Not only did Jesus stop to discuss this woman's salvation, but most believe He actually made a specific trip with His followers, through this area, just for such an occasion. It was on this specific stop that Jesus shared "living water" with this woman, who later told the members of her community to "come see a man who told me all the things I have ever done. Is this not the Messiah?"

Jesus clearly seized many organic opportunities to create maximum impact with the men and women that followed Him during His Earthly ministry. His lifestyle ought to impact the lifestyles of His modern-day followers, as well. If you are too busy to stop along the way, to make time for those around you, you are too busy, indeed. It is not only those who look like us, think like us, and act like us who are worthy of our love and attention, but also those who are polar opposites to our respective people groups.

When we take the time to seize these impromptu opportunities, we are walking in the footsteps of our King. Regardless of the outcome, I can assure you that impact can and will happen.

In 2005, I traveled to Nashville, Tennessee, with a group of college students. Upon arrival, we walked the streets with an extra bounce in our steps. If you looked closely, you could have seen the glow of country stars in our eyes. We spent the weekend bouncing from live music venue to live music venue, trying on Cowboy boots, eating good food and making memories together. We must have walked past a hundred, or so, homeless men and women on the streets, during our stay there, but the last day, something different happened.

As I walked past a gentleman sitting on a bench at a bus stop, something kept me from just strolling by, this time. A couple of friends and I stopped to chat with him. He was incredibly quiet. He was not begging for anything, just sitting there with his hands folded in his lap and his head down. I sat next to him. "My name is Joey," I said softly. "What's yours?" "Clarence," the man replied. And then he looked at me with the brightest blue eyes I believe I have ever seen to this day. "My friends and I were about to walk into this convenience store and get a bite to eat and we wondered if you'd like to join us?" "Yes," said the man. He picked up his bag and we walked around the corner into the store. "Get anything you want," I told the man. He picked out 2 hotdogs, a soda, and a bag of Doritos. Then we sat on the curb outside and ate our meals.

After we were finished, I asked the man if he would share his story with me. He did. He spoke of unfortunate circumstances that had put him on a path to being estranged from his family, losing his job, and then his home. He told me that he was trying to get to his only remaining family member in hopes that, one day, he could see his son again. I listened, and his story moved me.

I asked the man if anyone had ever taken the time to share the good news of Jesus with him. He told me that he had attended church a time or two, with his grandmother, but no one had shared the story of Jesus with him. I shared the story of scripture with Clarence that day. I started in the beginning, with Adam and Eve in the garden, and ended with John's account of a new Heaven and a New Earth that was being prepared for those of us who believe in the promise of God through the death, burial, and resurrection of Jesus. As I got to the part about Jesus' death at the hands of angry men, Clarence's big blue eyes filled up with tears. As I continued with the story, the tears flowed down his face. At the end of the story, I asked Clarence if he would like to place his faith in Son of God and he said yes! I held his rough, calloused hands, and we prayed together. That day, Clarence asked Jesus to take away his sins and he became a brother in Christ.

After sharing in this life-changing moment, I asked him if he would take the bus to see his family member if given the opportunity. He answered, "Of course!" But, then, his head dropped as he explained that he didn't have the means for such a trip. I asked him to hold on a minute and I pulled my friends away for a side bar conversation. "Would you guys be willing to put some money toward getting him to Cincinnati to see his family?" "Yes, we would love to help him!" We asked Clarence where the nearest bus station was located, and he told us that Greyhound was only six or seven blocks away. We asked Clarence to grab his bag, and we told him that we wanted to check on the price of a ticket. Enthusiasm entered his speech once again. "OK, absolutely, I'd love to!"

As we neared the station, I asked the guys to hang with Clarence while I went inside. I went to the register and priced the ticket. $63. My goodness, this is cheap, I thought to myself. We can change the trajectory of a man's life for $63?

"But you can go first class for $77." The lady behind the cash register said. The bus leaves in 2 hours. "Wait one minute," I told her. I got Clarence and my college-aged buddies, and we went back to the counter. "One first class ticket to Cincinnati, please!" Clarence's eyes opened even wider. "You're going first class today, Clarence." We purchased the ticket and Clarence settled into the station. We said our goodbyes and even got a great hug from our new friend, prior to leaving. To this day, we have never seen the man again. However, I am looking forward to the day when those big blue eyes meet mine on the other side of eternity. I can't wait to reconnect with Clarence in the presence of Jesus. It will be a glorious reunion.

In Christ, we have been given a first-class ticket to a life that we have only previously, dreamed of. His sacrifice, on our behalf, paid the price for a full and abundant life. Keep your head up, adventurer. There are those on the journey who are in desperate need of good news, and you hold the ticket. This is maximum impact, and it is only possible through a close proximity with Jesus. And when it happens, it will not only change others in close proximity, but it will mark your life, and your DiscipleTrip, forever.

Chapter 9: Everyday DiscipleTrip

"Contrary to our superficial thinking, there never was a distinction in his mind between home and foreign missions. To Jesus it was all world evangelism." - Robert Coleman, The Master Plan of Evangelism

MANY OF US, MYSELF INCLUDED, have gotten so revved up about a mission trip, ministry, or even Bible study that we have placed the well-intended, Christ-centered "thing" above the Christ-centered life we are to be living with those right in front of us.

It's easy to shift our focus to concentrated mission, over everyday mission. Some of my most impactful "God moments" came during times of focused service and worship, in other parts of the country and world. There's nothing quite like having a specific plan for impact. Many times, in the months leading up to such a trip, dozens of directed prayers are uttered for the people that may cross our paths during the trip. We pray for the Holy Spirit to guide our lives during these times and to alter the conversations that will be had. We pray for people to come to know God through His Son, Jesus, and to have life-changing encounters with the star-breathing Creator. We often implore friends and family members to join us in our endeavor, by committing to prayer and even financial assistance. The evening before the trip; I often find it hard to sleep, expressing the same eager anticipation as a child on Christmas Eve. Our bags are packed, and we are ready to go!

It is in these times that we can almost *feel* God at work in our lives. Sometimes, it's even like He's holding our hand and gently guiding our every step. "Say hello to this guy." "Stop and make time to talk to this woman." "Don't go there," the Spirit nudges. At the close of a mission trip, everyone on the trip comes together to debrief, share stories, read scripture, and even sing together. It's almost a little sliver of Heaven, right there on Earth. Then, the mission trip concludes, and the stories begin their slow fade toward a forgotten past.

What if I told you that "mission" doesn't have to happen that way? What if there was a way to live out the stories, that we so desperately long to experience, without having to wait until the next mission trip? What if the mission trip could start today and never end?

This is exactly what Jesus had in mind for His disciples when He gave them the Great Commission in Matthew 28. His operative command was to share the good news of His death, burial, and resurrection with those we come in contact with, *as we go* throughout our day. He did not instruct His church to make this an isolated task, that occurs one week out of the year, and then simply return back to our normal lives. No, instead He was instructing His followers to take their normal lives and live it on mission. In the words of Charles Spurgeon, we are called by Jesus to "stamp eternity on our eyelids." We are to view our everyday lives, our sense of "normal," with the kingdom of God in mind. We are to leverage our networks, in the here and now, for His eternal glory.

When we begin to view everyday as a mission trip, life starts to explode with color, added meaning, and previously-unseen purpose to seemingly trivial matters. Matters, like shopping for groceries, taking a trip to the park, or even walking around our neighborhood, gain the utmost importance, because we are living a mission trip. The men and women we come in contact with begin to matter to us, because they matter to God. When we have been changed by Jesus, we become conduits of God's grace.

For the follower of Christ, every day is a DiscipleTrip. Every morning begins a new opportunity to see God move. Each moment is brimming with opportunities for transformation. Each conversational exchange is an open door for Good News.

God is at work all around you. In fact, scripture tells us in, Acts 17:26, that He made, from one man, every nation of mankind. He made them to live on all the face of the earth, having determined allotted periods and the boundaries of their dwelling place, that they should seek God; and, perhaps, feel their way toward Him and find Him. Yet, He is, actually not far from each one of us. The problem is that we rarely take notice of His work and presence in our lives. When we pause to pray, reflect, observe, and listen to what He is revealing to us, our spiritual eyes begin to open, and we can live with eternity stamped on our eyelids. As followers of Christ, we have a unique opportunity to join God in His redemptive work in the everyday ebbs and flows of life. Should we attempt to reduce our interaction with the Father to "Sunday morning" or "mission trip" experience, we risk missing out on some of the most exciting opportunities to see the Holy Spirit at work in the mission He's already placed us on.

SURF TEXAS

In 2013, my wife and I moved to Dallas, Texas. During that year, we watched the Mavericks play basketball, the Rangers play baseball, and visited the Cowboys' stadium. Although I love to watch and play sports, I get even more excited about action sports. Wakeboarding and snowboarding are my absolute favorite activities, on this planet. Naturally, when I heard a friend, in Dallas, describe an indoor surfing facility that existed inside the Galleria Mall, I had to give it a shot. We loaded up the family, the next Thursday evening, packed our swimsuits, and set out for adventure. What I experienced, next, was something I will never forget. When we showed up, we discovered a man-made wave that was constantly propelled from a large wave generator. Surf instructors were on hand to help beginners get the feel of surfing and experience the thrill of standing up on the water, with two feet squared, firmly, on the smooth, handcrafted board. It took time to get used to the manufactured set up. Unlike the ocean, there was a firm, shallow floor just a few inches under the base of the wave. Overall, it was a cool experience. We left as indoor surfers, having conquered an indoor wave during the Texas winter.

SURF JACO, COSTA RICA

In 2009, my wife and I went with a group of friends to Costa Rica. Each morning, we woke up to open air windows and 70 degrees. It was glorious. That week, we had the opportunity to spend time in an orphanage, passing out Bibles, visit a more remote part of the country to paint a place where locals gather to worship Jesus (where we picked up a three toed sloth-one of the most fascinating animals I have ever encountered), and hand-mixed concrete to pour a foundation for a library. After a full week of hard work, blood, and sweat, we decided to spend a day at the beach.

This particular beach is well-known among the locals as a prime spot among the surfing community. The crystal-clear water and epic wave size make Jaco feel like a scene from Tom Hanks' movie, *Castaway*. Let me be clear, I am not a surfer. But I have spent just enough time on a surfboard to know that you want something between your chest and the wax on top of any surfboard or the chafing will debilitate you; and that's near the extent of my surfing knowledge.

That particular morning, the sun was peeking over the horizon, and we couldn't get into the water fast enough. We grabbed our rented surfboards and plunged into the ocean. We paddled out across the rolling waves and once we got past the riptide, we sat upright on our boards and waited. And we waited. And waited. We waited on our wave. During a couple of occasions, we grew impatient and attempted to ride a few smaller waves into the shore. A time or two, we got to the place where we could stand up, but our skill level prevented us from riding the smaller waves all the way in. That's the thing about surfing the ocean. It requires patience. You never know when the perfect swell is brewing beneath the surface.

After an hour or so, something began to change. The ocean was changing underneath us. It was hard to describe, but you could feel it. Larger waves were coming. White caps began appearing, as the waves broke over to form perfect tunnels. The intensity of the waves was increasing all around us. Three feet, four feet. This was reason the locals chose Jaco.

Clayton, my friend and co-adventurer, and I, began to paddle inland, as a particular wave approached us. This was the wave we had been anticipating. We paddled, feverishly, as the base of the curve slid under our boards. We stood up, near one another, just out of arms reach. Yes! We continued to ride the curl into the shallowing waters, and, then, with a *crash,* the wave broke. It barreled me, chest first, into the sand bar. I held my breath, felt the pull of the strap that connected the board to my body, and waited for the oxygen in my lungs to carry me to the surface of the ocean.

I heard Clayton moan as he came up from the whitewash. He had also taken quite a blow. One half of his surfboard surfaced. Then the other half. The wave had crashed down so hard on him that it snapped his surfboard! He picked up the pieces of his board, I carried mine under my arm, and we walked onto the beach. It was that afternoon that I gained a new understanding of the power of the ocean.

When I first began writing this manuscript, I had the idea that this chapter might have been some sort of outline for what a five-to-seven-day DiscipleTrip would look like. God has discipled me, greatly, in this process. He doesn't want our seven-day DiscipleTrip. He wants our everyday DiscipleTrip.

When we enlist in everyday DiscipleTrip, we step out of the manufactured safe zone of Christianity and into the wild and powerful forces surrounding the kingdom of God. But, do not fear, the God of the universe is at your side. Just like the surfing instructor, He will guide your misstep, and correct you, should you stumble. And when we embark on this journey in the community of others, we help one another when the waves of life – "natural" or "man-made," seek to ravage our souls.

Chapter 10: Road Blocks

I STILL HAVEN'T FORGOTTEN his words. "You are unfit for ministry," Tony snarled, as he began to air his grievances with me. Even though it has been 13 years since I heard those words, this old wound continues to haunt me. This was a statement proclaimed over me in my younger days when I was still highly unprepared for the road ahead. This memory serves as a reminder that I have been on the receiving end of failed discipleship.

Thankfully, I have also been blessed to be on the receiving end of discipleship, done well. One such example took place in 2017, as I had dinner with Neil Cole; one of the men whose work inspires me. At this time, I was five months into a backyard conversation about Jesus with a group of a dozen or so, irreligious friends that I had met surrounding the game of golf; a passion that we had all shared. My time with these men had been a journey; one in which I felt as though I was learning how to follow Jesus all over again, while attempting to teach others to do the same.

As I took the next bite of my John Daly, Big Boy, burger, I wondered if I was even making sense of my words. My dinner partner, Neil, and his seminal work, "Organic Church," caused me to think differently about the life and teachings of Jesus for the first time in my life. "When good seed meets good soil, growth happens, and there's nothing you can do about it." At the very mention of this concept, I was reminded that the pressure to perform is off and the word of God is powerful. "Just listen to Jesus and do what he tells you," Neil reminded me, as I inquired about my next steps in attempting to make disciples of this group of men that God had strategically placed in my life. Neil Cole taught me the organic road to discipleship.

EXCESSIVE WEIGHT

During the process of attempting to fulfill the Great Commission, given by Jesus to the Church, I have simply dropped the ball. I have begun the process of helping others follow Jesus, only to begin the relational drift away, after a period of months. This can happen for a number of reasons, some of which are out of our control.

I would argue that it is primarily not the job of the man or woman who is walking another person down the road of sanctification to consistently and routinely monitor their disciple's spiritual progress. I believe it is the obligation of every follower of Christ to "keep their own tank full" rather than to rely on another person to fill their tank. Those seeking to be guided by another should be responsible for pressing in to the relationship, not vice versa.

The process of becoming like Christ, and helping others do the same, is often painful. It is also important to note that this process rarely feels spiritual. God seems to use the difficult times to chip away at our rough edges and reveal our desperate need for Him, through our weaknesses. Sometimes, the mountaintop experiences can last for weeks and the valleys can seem endless, often lasting months or even years. I have a bad tendency to spread myself too thin, relationally, and attempt to accomplish too many tasks in an effort to point others to Jesus. During this particular season of my life, I am attempting to coach a little league baseball team, connect with a dozen men through playing recreational league softball, shepherd other pastors throughout the state of Arkansas, not to mention love my wife and kids. I also forgot to mention that all of those items listed were attempted today. What profits a man to gain the whole world but lose his soul? When misplaced, my desire to help others follow Jesus, actually becomes a lesson in pretending that I, myself, am the Messiah. This never ends well. I have discovered that I make a terrible Savior. In these times, I have failed to love my wife, well, and have neglected the soul care of my own children. In turn, I have provided a bleak misrepresentation of Jesus to the those I am attempting to disciple.

It's Friday, and I had been looking forward to a combined date night with some close friends and had even arranged three hours of childcare. However, my attempt to be Jesus, rather than to simply point others to Him, had led me to a not-so-kind exchange of words with my bride, which ended up with me napping in the other room, during the time that we had set aside to connect with one another. Please hear me when I say, there are times when the process is not pretty. We have made our apologies and I am confident that God's mercy will be new in the morning.

I once heard a former lifeguard speak of his experiences in attempting to guard the public from drowning in the part of the oceanfront beach that he helped to oversee, in Southern California. He told me that there were two types of people that were the most difficult to save. The first were those that were clearly being pulled to sea by the riptide. Upon swimming out to rescue, these prideful chaps would attempt to convince the trained professional that they were fine swimmers, in no need of assistance. Unfortunately, the lifeguard is unable to help someone who is convinced that they are fine on their own. The second group was much different. They represented those who desperately wanted to be saved but would fight the lifeguard by flailing their bodies onto the rescuer, attempting to climb on top, often resulting in an intense physical struggle. If the lifeguard attempted to save the drowning individual without a life saver, this approach could be fatal for both parties. The lifeguard said that the key to saving this type of individual was to offer the life saver as a floatation device, rather than sacrificing his own body, as such. However, if the panicking victim continued to insist on climbing the lifeguard as a rescue device, there was only one way to divert the victim's attention. The lifeguard was trained to hold his breath and dive underwater, himself. The victim would immediately release his grip on the man, and the lifeguard would then swim a few feet away, pop up, and offer the device to the drowning victim. This process would be repeated until the victim learned to use the device rather than to use the person.

There have been so many times, in my experience in disciple-making, that I have been used as a flotation device. This process rarely ends well and can damage both myself and the person I am attempting to disciple. I am learning to hold my breath, dip under water, and attempt to offer the life saver instead. Jesus is the saving mechanism, not me. I make for a very poor flotation device.

MOLD IN THE FLOORBOARDS

In preparing for our own family DiscipleTrip, we did one of the craziest things I think we could do. We found an old, 1977 Volkswagen Westfalia Campmobile, online, and went to see it with a bunch of guys from the church. The next thing I know, we're towing the thing to my house. There it was, sitting inside my garage, in all its glory, with two flat tires and crud so thick on the outside, you could barely know the actual color of the van. It hadn't moved in two years. As I stood back, with my wife, and looked at this thing, it became clear that this was a huge project that was going to require great investment before we set foot on the road.

To our surprise, and thanks to the ridiculous talents of four amazing guys from the church, we ended up being able to drive the old girl into town, the next night, for dinner. She was a barely cleaned up version of her mess, but she was running. We were celebrating the surprising fact that she had, visually, been redeemed.

The next day, the guys came back over to take another look. And then we found it. Mold in the floorboards. Deep. We're not talking a replace-the-carpet-kind-of-situation. We're talking major demo, deep clean removal; serious time and significant investment. The excitement, from the evening before, took on its own flat tire when we realized our perceived treasure had just gotten all the more expensive.

In other cultures, especially in past times, men typically paid a "bride price" for their wives. It was actually a sum of money that was paid to the parents, or father-of-the-bride, in order to obtain the daughter in marriage. If the church was always the Bride of Jesus, then certainly our "price" went up dramatically after sin entered in. Our redemption, at that point, would be the highest price of any.

And here is where we are faced with a decision. The reality of most of our lives is that there is mold under the floorboards. Nobody knows our condition more closely than Jesus; the One who had to pay the true cost of the redemption. We might be able to walk the walk, even make our way to a nice dinner (or ministry or service) looking the part, but our ongoing restoration occurs at the deepest of levels, where it requires the most from the workers. The investment deepens, the time multiplies, and the spirit is tested. But the cost is way too high for us to leave the mold there; festering and multiplying itself in the dark. In fact, the cost of leaving it there can cost us our lives. Mold poisoning, just like sin poisoning, can be deceptively toxic to those who aren't aware of all its implications and symptoms.

So, on this trip, be prepared to find mold in the floorboards, and realize that it may not only change the course of the entire trip and way you travel, but the true investment needed in the long term. And that will usually come with some fallout. When the rubber hits the road – or in this case, the floorboards need to be ripped up, the van gutted and everything needs to be rebuilt and made new – there are very few people who will be quick to raise their hands to volunteer to overcome the roadblock. Will you be willing to do so, for the treasure that is the created being sitting next to you? Would you want someone to do it for you? Weren't you worth enough to be redeemed at all costs?

Put the gloves on. Get in for the long-haul. Rip up the floorboards.

DETOURS

I recently went on a trip where everything was pre-planned, for the five of us that were going. It seemed like a true blessing when all came together with transportation arrangements, housing, and even a packed schedule of activities for each day. In preparing for the trip, I knew it would be an adventure, but I had a preconceived notion of that adventure based on the plans I had made.

On the very first day of the trip, the day of our arrival, we hit a major, unexpected detour. The housing we had secured for the week was no longer an option. While the details aren't important, we knew that God had purpose in what seemed like a significant inconvenience and potential financial hardship. We had to rethink and reconsider the many days of activity that would now be affected by a change in location.

In less than a few hours, we were able to secure another option, which would cut the trip short by a few days, but would allow for some of the activities we had already planned. We rearranged some plans and cancelled the others that didn't make the cut, and trusted that God had His hand in it all.

On the last day of the newly arranged trip, a day which originally would have only been the third of seven days, God brought the five of us to a special place, where the youngest of our crew heard the Shepherd's call and came to his knees in repentance, receiving salvation. His was the only, of all of our hearts, that had not yet submitted to Christ, prior to this moment. When this happened, we peacefully looked at one another, knowing that how it had manifested was all planned with purpose. We all felt closure in that being the final purpose of our trip. We headed back home that night.

Understanding God's detours, and even the road blocks, is one of the greatest gifts we are given, as believers. This gift does *not* come with every detour or road block, though. It's in the occasional glimpse of understanding that we realize the attention our Father has on every detail from the beginning to end. And when we arrived home, we found a friend – unexpectedly visiting from out of town -

that needed the attention and care of our crew on the very next day. We wouldn't have been there for him if God didn't rearrange; all to the good of those who love Him (Romans 8:28).

Chapter 11: Unexpected Travelers on the Road

THE WORD TELLS US that our thoughts are not His thoughts and our ways are not His ways (Isa 55:8). So, much of our DiscipleTrip should, in fact, be filled with surprises and unexpected outcomes. Some of these surprises will bring laughter and unexpected joy, as you'll see at the end of this chapter, and others, unexpected hardship. When the relationships we invest in dearly take unexpected turns and our discipleship efforts don't seem to pan out, we can be left really bewildered and seemingly stuck.

Such was the case with my own grandfather. On my DiscipleTrip with him, I had a very different plan in mind. I expected a certain traveler on the road, and my seemingly God-aligned plan did not happen as I expected. However, I hope that you can discover that, sometimes, our view of discipleship can be short-sided. Our vantage point is limited, in the grand scheme of the kingdom.

I always knew that my grandfather was a harsh man. My first memory of Billy Cook involved sitting with him on the front edge of my great grandmother Ruth's front porch of her house trailer. The sun was out, on this particularly beautiful day, and food was cooking inside. The roses were in bloom, in bright red clusters, surrounding the large wooden area with the fragrant smells of early summer in the Ozark Mountains of northern Arkansas. The birds sang to the passing clouds, that swept their way across a blue sky. We were swinging our legs back and forth, as my Papaw spit into the grass in front of the porch. Feeling like a big boy, I couldn't have been more than 8 at the time, I followed suit. As soon as I worked up enough spit in my mouth, I let it go forward. To our misfortune, my spit hit the top of his boot. I will never forget the look that came over his face. His face immediately scowled, and even seemed to glow red, and he began to hurl insults my way. I didn't know what the rest of the words meant, at the time, I just remember it starting with the word "You …" He reached back and I flinched, knowing for certain that I was about to getting slapped for my misbehavior. Instead, he stormed into the house and slammed the front porch door, as his harsh comments turned to mumbling and eventually drifted into the house.

As I have grown older, I learned that this type of behavior was more than common, and I'm not certain that my grandmother was so fortunate as to simply flinch at his raised hands. I'm betting that those hands found their way to their target, more often than not. But who am I to judge a man who lost his oldest son, a teenager at the time, to the Vietnam war? His second oldest, my father, had a tragic motorcycle wreck that same year, claiming his left leg in the accident.

Fast forward to 2012. On this particular day, I was speaking at my great Grandmother's funeral. A woman who faithfully served the Lord until the end of her life. She was on my mother's side, and the only thing I could think of, as I spoke of her faith, was my angry grandfather who had never experienced the grace and love that only Jesus can give. Immediately after finishing my speech, I walked out of the back of the country church, where the funeral was being held. As I got into my 1992 Red Honda Civic to drive to my grandfather's house, tears began to stream down my face at the thought of Papaw Cook going to Hell for eternity. I cried out to God, "Please, save my grandpa. Please open his heart, mind, and eyes to your grace." Looking back, I'm certain it was God's grace that protected me as I yelled out, wiping tears with my sleeves throughout the 15 minutes that it took to arrive at his house.

As soon as I knocked on his door, Papaw Cook immediately and enthusiastically invited me in. We sat on his vintage brown, plaid couch, and he asked me what brought me to his house today. I told him that I needed to tell him something. "What is it?" he curiously replied. "I came to tell you that Jesus Christ was a real man, born of God, to woman named Mary. This Jesus lived a perfect life and died a terrible death at the hands of angry men. Jesus didn't stay dead, but the Bible says that his grave burst open three days later and that He conquered death. Jesus told His followers that He could bring eternal life if only we would believe in Him, repent of their sins, and trust Him as their Savior." "Joey," my grandpa said, "you're a good man, and your mom and dad are good people too. I'm so proud of you and your dad. You have grown up so well, and I am really thankful for the way you both help people. But I am not like you. I am a bad person who has done lots of bad things." In a desperate plea to prove to my grandpa that I was not "good" like he thought, I walked out of the living room and into his kitchen. "Where are you going?" he asked. "To prove you wrong." I reached into his refrigerator and pulled out a can of Old Milwaukee beer. My papaw drank so much of the stuff that he had earned the nickname, Old

Billwaukee, from his drinking buddies. Much to his surprise, I popped the top and began to chug down the contents of the can. I was 30 and this was my first taste of beer, and somehow, it was in response to the Gospel of Jesus. "I told you, Papaw Cook, I am not a 'good' person." I clearly remember thinking this must be what cat urine tastes like. "What are you doing?" Papaw was shocked. "Your mom and dad are going to kill me!" I laughed in response, "I won't tell them if you won't." After the initial shock wore off, we sank back into my grandparents' couch to continue our conversation.

"Shortly after your dad lost his leg and my son, Stevie, lost his life, a couple of men in suits showed up on this front porch." He pointed to the front door which connected to the living room that we were sitting in. I noticed his countenance begin to change drastically. "They introduced themselves as pastors at the church down the street, but I already knew who they were. I sat them down on this very couch and they said they were here to bring me some bad news. They said they heard about what happened to my son Steve and that if I didn't get my life right, more bad things would continue to come to my family." At this point in the story, I could actually hear the grit of my grandfather's teeth as they ground together, while his jaw continued to tighten. He balled his fist together at the mere thought of these men. Through clenched teeth, he told them to get out of his house and to never come back. My heart broke at the thought of the distorted message of religion that had plagued my grandfather for the majority of his life. I wept in front of Papaw Cook that day. I apologized on behalf of the men who lied to grandpa; not only misrepresenting the God they thought they knew, but also grossly misunderstanding what God had accomplished through Jesus's sacred pilgrimage to Golgotha and back to Heaven. "Hypocrites," he said. "All hypocrites." I agreed with my grandfather's sentiment. "Yes," I replied. "We are all hypocrites. All of us who follow Jesus

110

pale in comparison to His goodness. But that doesn't change the fact that His grace and love are perfect and available to all of us hypocrites." "I wish I could believe it, Joey," my grandpa said.

Those words still ring in my head as I type these words from my downtown, upstairs office years later and miles away from the old Cook homestead. "I wish I could believe it."

We talked for another hour. We pressed into the nuances of the Bible that he simply could not believe. We talked about what he read over the years through his National Geographic subscription, television programs that had "disproved" the existence of a divine creator, the age of the Earth according to science, and even a short stint on aliens.

"You almost persuaded me to be a Christian," King Agrippa told the Apostle Paul in Acts, chapter 25.

A couple of years after that talk, my grandfather asked me to pray for his upcoming surgery. I did, and his health continued to decline. We buried my grandfather in 2016 on a rainy, August day. It was difficult to do the funeral. I struggled to find words of hope. The red clay mud was caked onto my boots, that evening, when I finally made it home. Lost in the mud, I couldn't make heads or tails of this. Until I found an unexpected traveler on the road.

Little did I know that my grandma had been listening. And watching. For years she watched, and she listened. When no one was paying attention to the sweet lady, who always lived in the background, she was paying attention to us. Six months after my grandpa passed away, on March 12th of 2017, my Granny Cook repented of her sins and made Jesus the Lord of her life. April 23rd of 2017 was one of my favorite memories of all time. It is the Sunday when I had the privilege of baptizing my 83-year-old grandmother. After giving her heart and life to Jesus, she has never been the same. "My decision to follow Christ was influenced by the people around me," Donna says, regarding her decision to give her life to Christ. "It made me happy. Everything changed. It was like a burden was lifted off of my shoulders and everything was peaceful... Now, I have Christ in my life and I'll never walk alone."

To know Granny Cook is to love her. She brightens up every room that she enters. Her laugh is contagious and the dressing that she cooks at Thanksgiving deserves an award. If you ever get the chance to eat a meal with my grandmother, pray first. If you don't thank Jesus before you start eating, she may stop you and insist that everyone prays together before continuing the meal. Isn't it just like God to take our trivial efforts at sharing the Good News of His son Jesus and do exceedingly and abundantly more than we could ever ask, think, or imagine in the life of someone that we didn't even notice was listening?

I once stepped away from a phone call to talk with a couple of teenagers. During that conversation, I had the opportunity to share about what Jesus had done for them. Years later, the person who was on the other end of that phone call told me that I had forgotten to hang up, and, that day, she responded to the Gospel message I shared, by giving her life to Christ. You just never know how a paragraph might end or how Jesus might show up right in the middle of your mundane and do something supernatural.

THE LAST EXIT

Sometimes you just need to go the extra mile, to take the last exit. Relying fully on our plans can fail to put us in a place to experience the unexpected. Allow me to share one example that is sure to leave you laughing as it did us.

It was getting close to midnight on this particular evening, and we had taken a small group of guys to Little Rock, Arkansas, to experience some bro time, in hopes of growing our faith along the way. I find that no excuses are needed to get people together, even if it's just for the evening. This particular evening, we were going to visit some friends and eat at Waffle House, one of my favorite spots to hang. You never know what is going to happen at a Waffle House and the staff always seem up for conversation. We prayed together over our meal, talked about our relationships with significant others, told stories, and laughed. We always laugh. Not the kind of courtesy laughing that you do to make any environment smoother, but *real* laughter. For us, laughter is a sign of real friendship.

On our way home, we were caught up in the moment and we just wanted to be together a little bit longer, so we decided to take the last interstate exit back home. We were all riding in a 15-passenger van, to our favorite 90's sing-along music playlist, and we wanted a few more minutes together. On this particular evening, we noticed a truck pulled over, in kind of, a tucked away portion of the exit ramp, and its emergency flashers were on. Interestingly enough, it had two jet skis trailered behind the truck. We noticed a guy walking around the vehicle and slowed the van, as we quickly debated on whether or not we would stop and help. We decided that there were quite a few of us and there seemed to be only a couple of them, which gave us a sense of safety, should danger arise. So, we stopped. What we found out next shocked all of us, even to this day.

We first introduced ourselves to the man, now outside of his truck. "I'm Dr. Robert," said the man. "Nice to meet you," I said. Robert told us that he had accidentally put diesel into his unleaded truck and only made it a couple of miles before his large pickup shut down on him. We offered to help, and he was very thankful. Robert was in a bind, and we could all tell that he was ready to keep moving, even under the cover of night. We needed tools, gas, and a can in order to drain the fuel and replace it with the unleaded to get him back to the road. So, shortly after midnight, we loaded up the jet skis behind our van and Robert and his passenger were now riding with us on our way to Walmart for supplies.

Robert's passenger opted to stay parked in the lot with two of our guys in the van, and the jet skis. They had come to trust us in the van ride over, after discovering that we were followers of Christ, motivated to serve them through our faith. Myself and one other assisted Robert in shopping for supplies. As we were in the store, we realized the reason behind the passenger's desire to stay in the van.

"Did you recognize her?" Robert asked.

"No," we replied.

"That's Sunset Thomas," Robert said, almost proudly, as we shopped for a gas can. He could tell that I wasn't picking up what he was putting down.

"She's the most popular porn star in the world," he said.

"Oh," I said. "Wow." I didn't know if I was supposed to congratulate him, be embarrassed, or even pretend to know her in order to stay in his good graces.

"I saved her," Robert stated. "From a life of prostitution."

"She was being held captive at the Bunny Ranch and we are now on the run."

Suddenly, everything made sense. The urgency to get back on the road, Sunset's insistence on staying in the vehicle, and Robert's steady desire to protect his passenger all made sense now.

After getting what we needed, we got back in the van. During the trip back, we had an open dialogue about Jesus, Robert's faith, and Sunset's struggle to accept the truth of the Gospel that Carson had shared with Sunset while we were in the store; due to her life experiences and her issues with trusting men.

Once we arrived back at Robert's truck, we asked if we could pray over both Robert and Sunset and they quickly said that they would appreciate it. So, we did. We circled up and prayed right there with the most famous porn star the world had ever known and her rescuer.

After getting back in the van to head home, there were a few minutes of complete silence. No 90's playlist, no porn stars, no noise whatsoever. Just silence, holy silence. We all knew that we had just experienced something supernatural. God had ordained this encounter and we all knew it. It felt like the scene from the movie *Stand by Me* where the now, inseparable friends, walk home after their run in with fear, victory, sadness, and joy, in complete silence.

Before turning into my driveway, we all burst into laughter in unison. The thought of what we had just experienced was overwhelming and the only way to respond was to laugh out loud in astonishment. Sitting in our driveway, after both sides of our stories had been told, Carson confessed that he had just shared the Gospel with the first woman that he had ever seen naked. Our God is in the business of redeeming all of creation to Himself, and that had included us.

As you journey in your DiscipleTrip, don't forget to consider the last exit. You may just encounter Jesus there.

Chapter 12: Checking the Tires

NOT TOO LONG AGO, I woke up from a dream. It wasn't the kind of crazy, scary, or nonsensical dream that you realize later was illogical and ridiculous. It was a different kind of dream.

On this particular morning, I woke up with large hot tears flowing out of the corners of my eyes. It was a sensation that I never experienced before. The reason for the tears is what makes this story significant. I have recently been under quite a bit of pressure to perform in my current job. You might think it is strange to hear a pastor speak of his work as a "job," but bear with me for a moment. My "work" was getting heavy, and I was feeling the strain of the week closing out, as I woke to speak to a gathered crowd, waiting to hear from God through a Sunday sermon. But this particular morning was different. It was as if I had heard from the Lord. In fact, this *is* as close as I have ever been to hearing an audible voice from God. I would even go as far as to say that I experienced a "theophany" (Google that one later)! I didn't wake up to my alarm clock that morning, but to the feeling of a hand on my shoulder. It oddly felt as though my actual father was waking me up early in the morning with the words, "Get up son, it's time to go to work." After wiping the tears and coming to full awareness of the situation (you know the feeling of waking up from a realistic dream and realizing that you are actually in your bedroom), I sprang to my feet and practically ran to start the shower. As the water flowed over my head, a smile engulfed my face - one that I could not shake - at the realization of the new understanding that had come to me...

Today, I was going to work with Dad.

Do you remember what that was like? I sure do. There was only one such incident from my own childhood that I was able to remember. I remember getting in the truck that morning which was already filled with the tools needed for the day. Dad had packed us both sandwiches, chips and ice-cold Dr. Peppers to drink. Sure, we had a big day of work ahead of us, complete with manual labor, (pouring a concrete sidewalk to be exact), but did that really matter? Remember, I was a kid going to work with Dad! What a joy. It was in these waking moments that I realized that the bulk of my "ministry" was simply showing up! Dad would do the lion's share of the work. All I needed to do was hand Him tools and to do whatever He told me to do. What a liberating concept!

The results of our disciple-making efforts aren't contingent upon our proficiencies, gifts, or winsome personalities. Our Father is doing, and will continue to do, the work. Sometimes, all we need to do is to show up with a willingness to obey whatever God leads us to do.

So, relax; Dad has already checked the air pressure in the tires. In fact, His Spirit has filled them to the exact P.S.I. and will continue to serve as our guide throughout our DiscipleTrip.

So how do the tires of transformation turn? What does progress look like on this journey? These "Tires of Transformation" move through spiritual progress. The purpose of Christianity was never the accumulation of information, but rather transformation.

TIRE PRESSURE

BCF Ministries teaches an amazing example on this in their Self-Confrontation course. In the 1800's, a man named Samuel Plimsoll, had a major impact on the Nautical industry when he developed the way to account for the necessary load weight for ships to sail properly. Overloaded, ships were obviously in danger for sinking; trying to carry too much on their own. Underloaded, ships were improperly prepared against the wild waves and seas that were to come their way and they would inevitably get tossed – endangering everyone on board. Plimsoll developed the "Plimsoll Line" (now often referred to as the "water line" or the "load line") which is a line painted on the ship to show the level that the water should rise to on the outside of the ship, in order to ensure proper weight load; and thus, proper functioning.

There are, of course, great similarities to use in this example, especially in the journey of discipling others, but we would be wise to recognize that we are a faulty barometer for determining our own proper load level. We cannot be our own "Plimsoll Line." It is not our job to take on "ministry" or discipling efforts until we sink. It is not our job to stay away from carrying loads or helping to carry others' loads that initially seem too weighty. It is the work of the Holy

Spirit in our life to show us how to carry only and exactly what He's asked us to do, in order to operate as He's designed.

LOSING AIR – A PERSONAL CONFESSION

Paul said "Do not grow weary of doing good" (Gal 6:9). Jesus said His yoke is light, so we don't need to carry our own heavy one. We can just come to Him when we're weary (Matt 11:28). We have reassurance in Scripture to know that our Savior understands how easy it is to feel like there's just not enough air in our tires, and that the tread is feeling insufficient for the terrain.

I've chosen to write this section as I'm feeling that very same way. I'm worn. I do my best serving. I spend most of my weekends either serving my family, my church, or my friends. If not, I'm working – and that still is to serve. I am busy all of the time and I'm exhausted. Where is the time for me? I woke up this morning consumed by thoughts of what I want, what I perceive I don't have, and how I wish things were different. I am struggling to find joy, gratitude and contentment. I'm quickly getting irritated at everyone around me. There's a slow headache building up the back of my neck around to my forehead. I want to go back to bed and tell everyone that I'm taking the day off. It's never going to be enough, anyway. I'll never get done everything that needs to get done, fill everyone's needs, and make everyone happy. It will never be enough.

Right, wrong, or indifferent, this is the life of a Christian on the days that the tires are losing air. This is the life of a Christian because it is a life of a sinner, still in the flesh, battling against the powers and principalities of this world and all that our eyes see. Today, all my eyes see is that others don't seem to be struggling like this.

I considered not including this part in the book. There's nothing God-focused about my mood right now. I'm entirely self-focused. I can tell you all the Scriptures that apply to my complaints and negative thoughts. I can tell you how I know He will provide for my needs, sees all that I am doing and that serving Him is always worth whatever the price is that I pay for it. I know all these things. But right now, He also knows my mood. There's no hiding. He knows my thoughts. He knows I'm not feeling grateful, but resentful. I'm not in a Godly place and I'd rather hide. My heart is not right.

Did you ever have a bad day at school, as a kid – one of those where every single thing went wrong - and you came home and your mom or dad sat with you and had some milk and cookies? Honestly, I don't' specifically recall that exact scene in my own life, but that's the feeling I am seeking right now. As His kid, I know I can't run off and slam the door to my room and lock it, so He can't come in. He's already in there with me. I've learned enough to know that running my mouth at someone or proceeding in some sort of rebellious action is not the way to go and will only hurt more, afterwards. I am in that angry place of denial, where I want to be left alone feeling like "no one understands me" and desperately wanting to sit across from Him over a plate of milk and cookies and watch Him softly nod at me and say, "I get it." I barely have enough air to feel like I can press forward with the day, and, yet, I'm still supposed to keep giving and serving others. When do I rest?

Lord. Break through.

I'm not lovable in this place. I'm not worthy of any of your attention, Dad. Nothing I'm doing, thinking, or feeling in this moment represents You or the life You called me to when You adopted me. But the fact is, I'm hurting over all that's wrong in this world and in me. I don't want to do this anymore. I just want to stop. I want off, and I want, to just be with you.

This is the real, internal struggle of a disciple, and, if you are one, I imagine you can relate. I decided to include this part for that very purpose; to remind us, both, that we are not alone in this. Disciple. Apart from Him, we can do nothing. Nothing. (John 15:5 emphasis added). That means we cannot serve well. We cannot love well – *even* when people are being lovable. We definitely cannot love well when they're not. We can't be positive about trials. We can't be hopeful. We can't be strong, and we definitely can't find any sort of assurance in weakness. We can't even look like our "Christianity" brings us joy, because, without Him, there is no Christianity. If I'm feeling this dark, alone, hopeless, frustrated, I clearly am not feeling in proximity with Him. What a mistake. My feelings are deceiving me. He never left. I'm like a little kid pouting in the corner, unwilling to turn around and see my Dad there with open arms waiting until my tantrum is over so I can get the hug I need. The corner I'm staring at is my corner of the world which, right now, doesn't look loving, comfortable, or comforting to me at all. Lord, I need you. Turn my head, Dad. Turn my heart. Give me air. Remind me I'm not far. Remind me You never left.

Disciple, when you get this way… when you can relate… don't drive the car off the road. Don't keep driving until the tread wears bare. Just pull over. Stop. Rest. Rest in Him. And wait it out (Psalm 30:5). It doesn't last. Joy will come (Psalm 30:5).

The Ministry of Presence

When people go through periods of deep grief, others often wonder "what to say" during these difficult times. Frequently, our presence, alone, is much more powerful than our words.

Consider Job's friends. When all was lost, they came to be with him. They simply sat with him, mourned with him and were present for seven days. The problems between the group didn't start until they opened their mouths and started providing what they felt to be, and perhaps was well-intended, wisdom, in their own understanding. I think the beauty of this biblical example is that it reminds us that we can underestimate the power of the ministry of presence. Sometimes, we don't need to add anything else to it. Sometimes, just being there is enough to allow someone else to want to take the next step, the next breath, and find renewed hope.

Get Back on the Charger

My staff recently embarked on a DiscipleTrip to Lynchburg, Virginia. There, we attended a conference, shared meals, and even spent one evening snowboarding and tubing at a year-round, artificial ski slope. Our transportation for the week was an extended capacity Cadillac Escalade with all the bells and whistles. This vehicle was a thing of beauty! It even came equipped with wireless charging for your phone. All you had to do was place your device on the center console and boom, your phone was immediately charging. Our spiritual batteries function much in the same way. When we learn to rest, or abide, in the power of Christ (John 15:15), we are renewed! It is in the cross of Jesus that we find our rest. It's not in our good works that we are redeemed but in His finished work. The Gospel of Jesus has the power to save you in your wretched and sin-sick state, and also the power to "sustain you to the end, guiltless in the day of our Lord Jesus Christ" (1 Corinthians 1:8).

Chapter 13: Moving into the Driver's Seat

"… Jesus demonstrated so clearly in his day: that the multitudes can be won easily if they are just given leaders to follow." - Robert Coleman, The Master Plan of Evangelism

MY EDITOR, JOANNA SANDERS, shared the following story/insight with me: "Once in my early days attending church, after I had recently gotten saved, my friend saw my zealous eagerness to get to church on time and half-complimented me on my efforts and interest. She said that I would have to eventually stop going just to receive and start going to serve. I felt a little put-off, quite honestly. After all, I was 'a newborn,' barely starting to walk on my own. Why and how should I be expected to serve while I was still so new to the game?

I also backed up my posture with the phrase that I had heard so many others use in church, 'I'm going to get fed.' If I didn't go to church to get fed, then where else would I 'be fed?' And if I wasn't 'nourished/fed,' how would I serve someone else? Her direction, at the time, seemed a little contradictory.

As I continued to sit in the pew each week, I realized that I was comfortably doing so because of the others around me, who were doing simple things to make sure everyone else was comfortable. I was surrounded by the same people, serving others, as they had for me, when I walked in for the first time. They weren't doing extraordinary things. I didn't know how to necessarily spread the Gospel at that point, but I could, maybe, wash a dish. God wouldn't be offended, of course, by me getting there just a few minutes earlier to help set up some chairs. And He certainly would be served if I encouraged someone else or made their lives a little easier in some small way. I realized that I didn't need to start a new 'small group' and lead Bible study. I simply needed to show up, in small ways, and do something that I was already good at. I needed to bring one of my own gifts; not because it's just fun to give or do what you're already good at, but because it's what is required of us, as members of the Body (1 Cor 12:11-12).

We are required to get into the driver's seat simply because it's not fair or acceptable in God's eyes that we stay in the backseat the whole time. If you've been called to be a participant, and an heir, in His great inheritance, then you are called to participate in making disciples. Sometimes, we all have to take turns driving. Or setting up chairs. Or extending smiles. Work is pleasing in God's eyes, and when we're working with His mission in mind, it's the very best we can give. You don't need to drive well; you just need to be willing to try and trust Him. Let's climb into the front, today, and share, with a willing heart, how far He's brought us. The Spirit's got it from here."

WHEN DO YOU KNOW YOU'RE READY TO DISCIPLE SOMEONE ELSE?

You're ready. Let's explain why.

Discipleship, for too long, has been lost in some idea that it needs to be structured and measured. Sure, there are some great tools out there for structured discipleship and measured changes to gauge where we're at, (like the Tire of Transformation), but we are losing so much if we think that's all there is. Again, take it back to the very first DiscipleTrip. Absolutely nobody was a seminary-grad. The only requirement for the trip was willingness; a "yes," when Jesus prompted with "Follow Me." So, the only requirement for you to engage in that process with someone else is willingness.

Hopefully, by now, you realize that you do need the right tools to do the job and the critical one is the Word of God. Using your own "wisdom" (man does not have his own by the way – wisdom comes from God) will not be beneficial in discipling anyone; it will only lead them astray. Instead, using our own experience, matched and compared and directed to the Word of God, will lead them in the right direction. Remember, God can use anything, even the rocks (Luke 19:40), but He wants to use us! Your experience, as you learn, is valuable to share with others. As you talk with anyone in everyday circumstances, you can share your experiences in those moments, as well. The simplest thing to remember about Discipleship is that you take what you've experienced, learn from it, and tell it to someone else; pointing all the awesomeness to God.

So, if you've had any experience in being discipled, either by another Trip Mate or by the Holy Spirit, you are now a seasoned traveler! Let's consider what's happened to us, thus far, that transforms us from an amateur Trip Mate to a seasoned Trip Mate.

A buddy of mine once made a great comparison in his observation of an amateur rider versus a skilled, seasoned rider, on a mountain bike trek. He said he could always tell the amateur riders because they were the ones looking at the ground as they rode; making course corrections on the fly. The seasoned rider, he observed, was strategically predicting the next 1-2 turns up ahead and was preparing for them, based on his knowledge of the terrain. They knew, from their previous experience, how to look differently at the road ahead.

See, most of us are looking straight down and are unable to see the road ahead. When we live like this, we are constantly grinding gears in trying to make sense of our current, usually rocky, road or situation. Wisdom teaches us to keep our eyes up and fixed on the trail (or guide, Jesus), up ahead, so that we can make adjustments before they happen. Every DiscipleTrip you take should reveal new ways that you're developing, from being an amateur rider to being a seasoned traveler. And now, it's time to heed the call to help someone else start the same lifelong transformation. This trip is all about learning how to prepare and inspire others to embark on their own DiscipleTrip.

Each DiscipleTrip we take will challenge us in new ways. We will be tested. There will be times when we feel like amateur riders all over again. It's good to keep in mind that, just as this journey was not a straight, simple path from A to B, neither is any form of change. True change, in itself, is not linear. But His assurance for us is steadfast. He's got it planned and the path is good. Keep looking ahead and help others along the path as the various tests and bumps and twists and turns come up.

"BUT HE KNOWS WHERE I AM GOING. AND WHEN HE TESTS ME, I WILL COME OUT AS PURE AS GOLD." (JOB 23:10)

Chapter 14: Stories from the Road

I SEE IN YOU

On one of my first DiscipleTrips, I didn't know I was on it, and I certainly didn't think I was valuable enough to be on one. A brother decided to take me and show me a whole new perspective.

Two months prior to meeting with Chad, I was suspended from a Christian college. The drummer for our rock band had "borrowed" some old sound equipment from the department he managed, in order to "complete" our mobile set up. When the school confronted him about the missing equipment, we had already listed it on eBay in efforts to upgrade. Bad decision. The entire band registered for classes again the following semester, but I was too humiliated to return. Instead, I transferred to Arkansas State University, in order to finish my undergrad in business and try out for the golf team. It was now the Fall of 2004 and I had begun playing intramural sports with some guys that were a part of a campus ministry. The director of the ministry was in his 9th year as an Arts student, still in the process of completing his bachelor's degree. He set up a time for me to come by his office and offered to pray for me. When we sat down for this first time, Chad asked me to tell share my story with him. I spoke of the religious environment that I had experienced growing up and the struggles I had in reconciling my faith life with the promiscuous relationships that I had been in and continued to be involved in, at the time. I told him about being suspended last semester and how disappointed God must have been with me. Oddly enough, my failures didn't seem to negatively affect his response.

This was the first time I remembered hearing a sentence that began with the words, "I see in you." Honestly, I don't recall exactly what it was that he claimed to have seen in me, but I believe it had something to do with leadership potential. For the first time, it was as if I had an alternative on the table of my life, other than to simply fail, trying to live up to some unwritten standard of behavior. Chad not only believed in me, but he gave me access to his life. He set up a weekly prayer time for he and I to engage in meaningful conversation and began to include me on an occasional errand. I even remember having dinner with his family, in his home. It was so impactful to stand in his kitchen while he and his wife, Julie, finished preparing the meal and then sat down to pray and eat. At the time, it didn't really feel spiritual. Chad continued to include me on various activities, such as making a trip to the hospital to pray for a friend, barbecuing for the neighbors, and even bringing me along to sit in, what seemed to be, very important, "ministry-type" meetings.

During those couple of years together in that city, my life started to transform. I began to develop a heart that cared for the people that Chad seemed to care for. I still struggled with the same sexual sins, but something inside was changing.

132

The trip, Chad so willingly took me on with him in life, had sparked an interest in discipleship because I wanted to give others what he so "easily" seemed to give me.

- Joey Cook

THREE STICKS AND NO MAKEUP

My first camping trip turned into my first DiscipleTrip. I didn't embark with a group that purposely set out to do a DiscipleTrip; yet I knew the trip couldn't be without discipling one another since we regularly do it at home. But there is something to be said about a different setting that brings out a different side in people. And the element of time was essential. As many times as we had gone to each other's homes for a quick lunch, or out to get ice cream, there is something about having to travel and look out for one another over a period of time, in a variety of circumstances, that deepens bonds; especially since we are all busy working moms without a lot of time to spend together, outside of our daily responsibilities. The opportunity to travel was such a blessing, but the challenge in it was the deeper blessing.

Going camping, for me, made a significant impact as it took me away from any previous idea I had about "vacation." This was not a luxurious girls' weekend at a spa-resort. There was no luggage stand for my suitcase and there was no plush comforter. This was a close-quarters, $35/night cabin with five bunk beds, with no climate control, no mirrors (an important aspect for most women), and no bathroom. The bathroom, more than 300 feet away, through the woods, required that we incorporate "the buddy system," at all times. We washed pots and dishes among rocks, started fires in the rain, and had to get creative, as to how to share a pot of coffee with only a couple mugs. A racoon licked up our pots, one night, outside the cabin, after we bunked down. I have never vacationed with a racoon.

Just to make it a little more raw, my friend coordinating the trip informed us that makeup was not allowed. While I secretly loved this idea, it did bring me far out of my comfort zone. But there I was, sitting in my camping chair, rained out in my galoshes with no makeup, learning how to whittle for the first time and laughing until I cried.

For me, one of the most interesting parts of the trip came organically, during a forced day of complete togetherness in torrential rain. Instead of enjoying the lake, or hiking, or even just wandering about the campsite, we had two options: inside the cabin, or outside on the covered porch. I admit that I sometimes absolutely love being without options. So, my close friends and I sat on the porch, galoshes and all, and drank some coffee, while the rain saturated everything around us. During conversation, I realized that I had been playing with and peeling a small stick that I had found on the ground and had broken it into three pieces; each about an inch long. Even though it was all from the same stick, the pieces all looked different, despite their common elements. I smiled, as I felt an analogy coming on and my friends knew I was up to something.

In the next few minutes, we each talked about which one of the sticks we thought represented each of us, and why. We all agreed that the bark left on the sticks represented various levels of transparency and vulnerability of our walk with Christ. While we realized the conversation was pretty nerdy, it actually brought about some great insight into how we all saw one another. Realizing that we, sometimes, can get caught up in what's comfortable, it is easy to assume that we know how we seem to those closest to us. I now hold onto these three little sticks endearingly and will bring them on the, now confirmed, "annual" girls camping trip. While Matthew 7:1-5 talks about a speck and a log, these small sticks brought out that Scripture in a whole new way and provided a natural foundation for us to challenge and grow together.

- Joanna Sanders

GRACE

I grew up in a family that put the "funk" in dysfunctional. My dad drank himself to death when I was ten years old. His addiction destabilized our family. My brother went to prison nine times and I have no idea where he even lives now. My sister developed a crystal meth addiction that cost her custody of all four of her children. I was first introduced to marijuana when I was five years old. I was drugged and hopped around like a frog as entertainment for the stoned adults in the room. My dad was a drug dealer. I remember riding in the back of the car between two garbage bags full of weed. By the time I arrived in the roughest trailer park in Jonesboro, Arkansas, I had been exposed to abuse, sex, drugs, and crime. Once, I was given a white puppy and my dad came home drunk and grabbed it by the hind legs and slapped it dead across a tree. It was a rough childhood.

Then it happened. A little church down the road came knocking. A couple of brothers, named Mark and John ran a bus to pick up children and bring them to church. Mark would pick me up for a while, because for families like mine, it was free babysitting. I had no desire to go to church. We moved many times, due to finances and troubles and it would get me out of going to church. But through God's providence and Mark's day job of delivering furniture, he would find me. Once, I was outside in my yard, after several months of blissful church absence, when Mark drove by. I ducked behind the house and hoped that he did not see me. He delivered his stuff and then came to my door. He knocked and knocked and would not go away. Finally, I went to the door. He said, "Chad! I have been looking for you. I will be by Sunday to get you." He did not even ask. He just told me he was coming to get me.

Another time, I told our youth director that we were moving to a town south of Jonesboro. He did not even consider just letting me go. Instead, he drove 21 miles to get me and 21 miles to bring me to church. Then, he drove 21 miles to bring me home and 21 mile back to his house. He did that over and over. As I look back on that, it is a marvel to me. It was during those days that Doug shared his testimony with me and I was saved. I was 15 years old.

Over the years, God used that little church to put just the right people in my life to encourage my faith. Thomas, my Sunday school teacher, let me hang out with him on the weekends, when the alternative would have been real trouble. Wayne took me on his vacations, and his wife Betsy loved me in such a motherly way. Rusty let me use his car to take my driver's test. Larry took me hunting for the first time. Paul and Cheryl became our friends. Bryan prayed over me with such sincerity. Dale took me out and showed me how to witness and share the gospel. Our Pastor brought me to his house, and as I sat at his table, told me that as long as he had a place, I had a place and as long as he had food, I had something to eat. He took me in like a son. When I was in the eleventh grade, he asked me to consider going to college and told me he would pay my way.

Words can't do justice to how much I love the local church. It is the hope of the world, when it is done right. It was in that spiritual family that I found the Lord, my calling, my wife, and a hope that life might start off rough, but it can end well. The Bride of Christ is beautiful. The Lord gathers together a people to bring heaven down to earth. I was adopted into the family and will never get over the treasure that was invested in me.

Grace, that is the name of my home church. It's fitting.

- Chad Graves

ONE DISCIPLE

What I am about to share is, on the one hand, very exciting, and on the other, rather pathetic. It's about me making a disciple. The story is exciting. The pathetic part is the terminology, *a disciple*. You read it correctly...*a* disciple...just one. I have been so busy being a pastor, that I cannot remember when I actually took a lost person, led them to Christ, and discipled them...until Milo.

Less than a decade ago, I started a school. It is not a Christian school. It is a private school, built around the arts, and led by Christ-followers. The school is for children, ages two through elementary school, and it has been hugely successful, in terms of education and influence within our local culture. Most of the families involved do not attend church and have no intention of doing so. However, every year at Christmas, they all show up at our church; hundreds of them...to see little Suzy perform in the Christmas recital. Milo was one of those parents.

What started as a one-time event for Milo, became a weekly habit. He kept showing up on Sundays. I never met him during that time…never even saw him. But ninety days later, on Easter Sunday, he walked up to me and said, *"I have lived fifteen godless years, but today I have given my life to Jesus Christ."*

Here is the backstory. Milo grew up in a great church. He was so influenced by the church that he decided to go into full-time ministry. After high school graduation, he left for college to study for pastoral ministry. He joined a prayer group with twenty other young men who were also there to study for future ministry. However, the confusion encountered, at this very liberal school, was tragic. After several years of study and teaching, this group of twenty, to a person, declared that there was no god. And every one of them walked away from their faith. Thus, Milo's statement, *"I have lived fifteen godless years."*

Prior to this, God was already doing a work in my heart, related to making disciples. The simple plan shown to us in the New Testament had given way to the complicated church leadership structure that I was experiencing. And the results have been less than stellar. So, when I met Milo, I felt I had stumbled into a redemptive moment. I began to meet with him. It started slow. He is a very successful businessman, so my time with him was minimal. In addition, I did not have an agenda. Launching a discipleship program in Milo's life did not seem very life-giving. I just decided to try and be his friend.

Now, after two years, we have become great friends, and we have had many discipleship moments. A few months ago, he mentioned that his new life objective is to go back and lead his entire twenty-guy prayer group back to Christ. The first one caved shortly thereafter…nineteen to go.

But the Milo experience has changed me. In so many ways, I feel like I have become the disciple. In my years of ministry, I am pretty sure I have led a couple thousand people to pray to receive Christ. I am happy about that. But I am also pretty sure I have only discipled a handful of people, if you count my four children, and yes, I count them!

I have begun building a future that includes people who will never come to my church. And I have fallen in love with them. I am learning to talk to them and accept them just the way they are. They know I am a pastor, yet they don't feel pressure to come to my church. I just show up at their stuff, and they love that!

Don't get me wrong. I have not abandoned my church. I am just growing a new congregation outside the walls…filled with lost people.

If God gives me the time, I am giving the next twenty years of my life to this DiscipleTrip! I have no doubt it can be my best twenty years ever!

- Greg Wigfield

MY FIRST DISCIPLETRIP; WITH JOEY

I didn't know at the time, but my first experience with Joey Cook was in fact my first DiscipleTrip. My parents had recently divorced, and my father had gotten us involved in a large church down the road. This was my first real experience with "the church." I only attended because my dad made us. I stayed quiet in the back, too nervous and unsure of what was going on to start a conversation with anybody about anything. A few weeks in, Joey (along with his wife Syndal) showed up to take the position as youth pastor there. He walked in with a big smile and assured us that we were going to "have fun together." Having fun wasn't something I would've seen as a part of following Jesus, up to this point. Boy, was I wrong.

Joey knew that I came from a musical family and played a few chords on guitar, but, more importantly, he knew that I needed to be pursued. He knew that I needed to be loved. He knew that I needed to begin my adventure. He and a senior, named Ethan, the most popular guy in school, showed up to my house on a Wednesday afternoon. Keep in mind, there was nothing cool about me. I was a 14-year-old, insecure boy with an awkward haircut, given to me by a neighbor who "needed the practice." I didn't even know Joey knew where I lived. He asked my dad if I could hop in the jeep with them and head up to our Wednesday night youth gathering early. My dad could tell I was excited and Joey asked me to grab my guitar. I assumed they would like to hear the most recent love song I'd learned. Again, I was wrong. On the way to the church, struggling to hear with the wind blowing so hard with the doors off of the jeep, Joey told me I was going to lead worship that night. Lead what? Yeah, I knew how to play one K-Love song, but I didn't even know what leading worship meant. I immediately began to sweat and told them I couldn't. There was no arguing. We showed up early, got a sound check in, and I led our youth group in singing *"From the Inside Out"* which was *"The Good, Good Father"* of my day. It was one of the most uncomfortable days of my life, but, looking back, one of the most pivotal.

I'd never been intentionally sought out by anyone like this, other than family, and they have to. He actually *wanted* to spend time with me. Joey and I have now been in each other's lives for close to a decade. He's one of my closest and long-time friends, but it hasn't always been smooth-sailing. There have been several hills and potholes along the way, but isn't that the case with any road trip?

As a kid, feeling wanted and cared for by an older guy, like Joey, led to me placing a bit more faith in him than Jesus. I idolized him to an extent. I was a senior when he took me out to dinner and told me God was calling he and his family to Texas. We cried together, over our chicken wings. For four years, we had been walking together. When he left, I felt abandoned. I believed a lie that the previous four years were fake and that he must not have really loved me that much. At graduation, I looked out in the crowd for his face and didn't see it. It's true that we grow more in the valley than on the mountaintop. Through some pain, I actually started following Jesus and not just Jesus in Joey. It was beautiful. I was enjoying Jesus, growing, leading people around me, and even beginning to forget about the hole I felt when Joey left. Then came a detour on the road I didn't see coming.

The summer before I started my undergraduate at the University of Central Arkansas, in Conway, I worked as a laborer for a brick mason. On break, I went to my truck to drink some Gatorade and noticed I had a voicemail from a name I hadn't seen in nine months. I listened. In typical Joey fashion, he had some "very exciting" news he wanted to share with me. The rest of the day, at work, I was almost angry that he would reach out, now, as if nothing had happened; as if he hadn't hurt me. I'd reached out and he hadn't replied. I called back on my way home. Joey asked if I was going to UCA in the fall. I was. He preceded to tell me that God was calling him to plant a church in Conway, Arkansas, and that he would love for me to be involved. I gave him the Christian answer for no and said, "I'll pray about it." I had no intention of being involved in anything he was doing. Honestly, even on move-in day, I was hoping our paths wouldn't cross.

Guess who was waiting at Baridon Hall? Joey had a crew of 20 people ready to help me get all of my stuff to my room, in one trip. We caught up in my room and he prayed with my crying mom. I told myself, "It doesn't matter how nice he is, I'm not getting involved." I made it about one day before curiosity got ahold of me. I showed up to the house we had been given to start this City Church journey. I knew God was doing something special and I wanted to be a part of it, but I would have to tell Joey how I felt. We sat in the cafeteria and I let it all out. It was the first time I can recall being honest about the way someone had hurt me, in conversation. We cried, again, together. He apologized, and we picked up right where we'd left off on our DiscipleTrip.

Now we have been journeying together in life, loving people, and church-planting for almost six years. We've traveled the country, watched each other fail, watched each other succeed, and watched each other grow. Joey sat with my family when I graduated college. Joey let me cry on his shoulder, break-up after break-up. We've climbed Mt. Rainier and swam in the Pugent Sound with bioluminescent bacteria. We've shared Jesus with drunk neighbors, grumpy old men, and homeless people. We've baptized friends, laughed, and cried. We've competed in the National Air-Guitar Competition (yes, this is a real thing). We've seen Jesus give us favor in our city. We've fallen flat on our faces and gotten up. There's nothing special about Joey, but there is something *very* special about the same spirit that raised Jesus from the dead, that lives in us. A journey with Jesus is not about dreading a Sunday morning service. A journey with Jesus is a dangerous, awkward, exhilarating ride… but you've got to hop in the jeep, even if it makes you nervous. Joey and I have been on this DiscipleTrip together for close to a decade, and I hope to be on it for many more. I've never met a guy so gifted in taking people on a journey with him and Jesus. There will continue to be bumps along the way, but life is a journey and you weren't created to ride alone.

- Lane Long

Chapter 15: Live the Adventure

YOUR DISCIPLETRIP has already begun. Your mission is to take all that you have learned and apply it in the normal setting in which you operate. See, unlike the popular saying "what happens in Vegas stays in Vegas," a DiscipleTrip requires that nothing stays isolated to the trip – it all comes home in fresh application. Your new mission is translating your new adventure material to the adventure that you live on a daily basis. This, in itself, is a challenge. But as you follow Jesus, even the everyday adventures become a little more interesting. While God is unchanging, the life He asks us to live, for Him, is in a constant state of progression (Phil 1:6). You should be different than when you started your trip. What you are, today, may look different tomorrow.

DiscipleTrip is a trip that continues throughout your lifetime. It is a life with Jesus, making disciples *as you go,* that makes much more of a difference than a trip focused on Jesus, where the mission ends with the end of the trip. A DiscipleTrip is the journey of life that begins at the time you accept Him, until the time you are fully face-to-face with Him in heaven. You are to make the most of it by continuing along the cycle of self-reflection, as you did at the beginning, looking to make sure you've stewarded well what's already been given to you, before you seek out anything more, and being willing to take the adventure right in front of you.

If you've never journaled, this is an awesome time to start to record some of the work of His hand in your life. You may be more ready to do this than ever before, and believe me, you won't want to forget some of the adventures. You just "can't make this stuff up," as the saying goes. If you don't know where to begin, start the journal with the highlights of the DiscipleTrip you are currently on, the Trip Mates you're journeying with, and the things you are learning.

AVOIDING THE LOW

Have you ever gone on a mission trip or retreat, and come back on such a high, only to experience the inevitable low, afterwards, as you get back to everyday life? Hopefully, we've had such an awesome time engaging a DiscipleTrip that we do come back feeling "high," but we don't want those feelings to drive the next few days; otherwise, we will experience the pendulum, indeed, swinging in the opposite direction. In order to avoid the low, we have to be in mad pursuit of one thing: holiness.

You've likely heard the saying, "taking the high road." The pursuit of holiness is the high road. We're going to keep our eyes on the "high road" to avoid the low. When feelings drive, the low is, indeed, just that. That's how we will know if we allow them to drive, because we will start to associate with those "let down" feelings when the obvious part of the adventure has temporarily stopped, and the everyday routine comes in. But if we come home to that routine, on the hot pursuit of holiness, life will start springing up around us in ways we haven't experienced before. New adventures will be birthed as a result of following the Creator and letting Him create them right before our eyes. Our Father is watching to see if we trust Him to show us new adventure right where we are.

Remember the Tire of Transformation? The tire will always progress forward, as you pursue increased holiness. The Christian life on earth is about the pursuit of holiness – not the attainment of it. We are justified in Christ, but we are in a progressive sanctification process that completes on the day of Christ (Phil 1:6), so we cannot ever assume to have secured holiness in this life. We strive for it because He *is* it. (1 Peter 1:16). So, if you enjoy the chase, you'll be happy to settle in to this idea. We're hot on His trail, because it is the trail to the best adventure! Let's look for ways right around us, to take fresh perspective, fresh approach to the routine.

FOR THEM

The Bible says a good name is more desirable than great wealth (Prov 22:1).

When I started writing this book, my editor and I spent a lot time discussing the appropriate path for publishing and trying to understand the audience that God intended for this book. Deciding that it was all worthwhile for even just one soul to be touched by it was an easy objective. Even recognizing that it might just be for one person, we knew that it was likely going to still impact our families in one way or another. We set out to making sure that what we left behind in this book was something we'd be satisfied leaving to our kids – if it were the only book we got to write. We started to look at this as a tool to disciple our own kids, and that shaped the writing differently. The process of writing this book has discipled us in understanding the importance of a good legacy.

That doesn't mean we aim to enter onto a platform, have a certain number of social media followers, or "save" a certain number of people, (since we don't do the saving anyway). A good name is a reference of a good character. And everything we do, both personally and professionally, reveals that character. Who you are – or rather Whose you are – should not be different based on your environment. A disciple of Jesus is a disciple of Jesus to all ends of the earth, and that godly character should be visible in all areas of their lives. As such, that example reverberates throughout those around them – and most often through those that they are around the most.

The importance of a godly character trickles through generations we may never even get to meet. You may never go on a DiscipleTrip with your great-great grandkids, but you can be sure that the way you shape their grandfather, who shapes their father, will have a significant impact on them and the DiscipleTrip they take.

Consider the careful and intentional arrangement for the genealogy of Jesus, as seen in the first book of Matthew. The Bible names every generation, from Abraham to Jesus. God knew exactly what bloodline each of us would need to come from and what placement we should have in it to impact the ones to come in that same lineage. Think of that. There is something you and only you are supposed to do to impact your lineage. The exact length of time you will have to do so is already laid out, and there is a specific mission, along the adventure of the entire lineage, that only you are scheduled to accomplish. If that's not a DiscipleTrip, I don't know what is! We need to consider the importance of our actions now... because we simply cannot fathom the impact they will have on the next generation to come. Our next DiscipleTrip is all about the one to follow.

148

"Here is where we must begin just like Jesus. It will be slow, tedious, painful, and probably unnoticed by people at first, but the end result will be glorious, even if we don't live to see it. Seen this way, though, it becomes a big decision in the ministry. We must decide where we want our ministry to count – in the momentary applause of popular recognition or in the reproduction of our lives in a few chosen people who will carry on our work after we have gone.
Really it is a question of which generation we are living for."
- Robert Coleman, The Master Plan of Evangelism

Chapter 16: Debrief

AT THE END OF ANY JOURNEY lies an opportunity to debrief. The debrief is a time to unpack your bags, both physically and metaphorically speaking. During this time, the traveler takes inventory of his or her experience.

My hope, in sharing this perspective with you, is to describe the need for a movement of disciple-making, the potential for impact, a description of some of the things you might experience on your own DiscipleTrip, as well as some personal experiences that may even inspire you on your own journey. Allow me to illustrate the debrief, from my end.

Much in my own life has changed during the one, full year from beginning this project, until the time I am penning the final chapter. As you read the introduction to this book, you may have noticed that this project began in an attempt to engage a culture, including, but not limited to, the millennial generation, in the ancient art of disciple-making.

However, many discoveries have been marked along the way. For example, I have realized the vastness of the expanse that exists between believers' philosophies on discipleship and the actual percentage of people who are not engaged in practicing it.

ALARMING TRENDS

Of the 35 letters that I sent out for requests for real-life stories of disciple-making, less than one-third were returned. I am not suggesting that the pastors and leaders, (both locally and nation-wide), that I sent the requests to, have never made a disciple personally, but the responses alone have shown me that there is some lack of interest in sharing such stories. In February of 2019, the Barna Research Group released a study which claimed, "Almost half of millennials who identify as Christian, believe it is wrong to share their faith". This was one of the most alarming headlines that I have ever read in regard to Spirituality.

GOOD NEWS

You can impact this trend. Your engagement in this ancient art of disciple-making, based on the premise CPJ + CPO = MI, can, and will, alter the trajectory of your friend or neighbor's life, your classroom, your workplace, your community, or even your city. This has certainly been the case in my life, throughout this experience.

One of the things you will learn in this journey is that when you let God have sovereign kingship in your life, you will begin to expect the unexpected. Six months into this manuscript, I made a purchase that I'm not sure my wife and I ever imagined. I bought a 1977 Volkswagen Westfalia Campmobile. If you are unfamiliar with this particular model of automobile, simply flip to the cover of this book. When we purchased the "micro bus," or *Kombi,* as the Aussies call it, it had two flat tires, rust holes throughout, a door that was jammed, wasp nests embedded into the interior, chipping paint, decayed fabric, a hole in the dash, a dead battery, and a motor that had not turned over for five years. Needless to say, it required massive work. My travel companions guided me with a firm "no way," after initially viewing the vehicle in its native habitat, which was in the edge of a wooden mountainside, near a remote cabin in rural Arkansas. After taking a lunch break to think it through, myself and my surprised companions hand-loaded the American icon onto a U-Haul car hauler and took it to its new, suburban home. The restoration process began.

My Trip Mates, in this leg of the journey, consisted of a dozen or so men who have grown into cherished, and what I believe will be life-long friends, during this project. I had not known some of these men, prior to restoring the bus, that we now affectionately refer to as "Herschel," named after my great grandfather-in-law, who passed away just before this journey began. The restoration has taken longer than I planned, cost more than I budgeted, and is more fulfilling than I could have ever imagined. At one point, I even landed in the emergency room after a steel cutting blade exploded, during use, and required me to get 18 stitches inside and outside my lower lip. God has taught me many things about myself, and others, in this process. During another restoration session, and hours and hours into scraping paint off of the outside of the Kombi, God gave me a picture of the decay inside my own soul that He was removing, simultaneously, as I continued to learn to trust Him, during the "less than sexy" times of difficult work. Long before ever hitting the road in Herschel, it became clear that the journey of my own DiscipleTrip had already begun.

In the early days of writing DiscipleTrip, I received a text that my friend, Andrew, had been in a near fatal motorcycle accident. Andrew and I owned

"Cafe Racers," vintage Honda motorcycles that had been reengineered to become trendy and powerful road machines and would ride them together from time to time. Andrew's accident had a profound impact on my own life, not only as a friend, but also because of the memory of my own father, who had lost a leg due to a similar accident. That day, I rushed to the hospital and prayed for my friend who was laying on a stretcher, immobilized, garnished with fresh blood on his new hospital gown. He was bed-ridden for weeks. Andrew was not allowed to walk for months, following his injury. Many of the bones in his wrists, arms and legs had been utterly destroyed. He was placed on an experimental therapy to regrow his leg, based on the use of magnets. Andrew felt depressed, and for good reason, while his newly wed wife, Annika, was immediately forced into the role of caretaker and nurse.

One sunny Thursday, I texted Andrew and asked him if he wanted to get out of the house. He replied, "YES!" We loaded up his wheelchair in the back of Herschel, the Volkswagen Westfalia, and set out for an afternoon of adventure. It was glorious. Our friend, and fellow trip mate, Joe Poulson, followed us, that day, in his truck, and was even kind enough to snap the picture that was used on the cover of this book. The whole experience left me with a sense of God's love and presence, in a fresh way, that I had not previously experienced. The amount of satisfaction that you will receive when you serve and love others in the name of Jesus is nearly overwhelming. That day, I developed a "perma-grin" that must have stayed on my face for at least a couple of days!

THE HIGH COST OF STICKING YOUR HEAD THROUGH THE FENCE

As a kid growing up in the country, I could look out my bedroom window and see rolling grassy hills outlined with fences designed to hold livestock. I would watch as the cows would stick their heads through the barbed wire fence to eat the grass on the other side. I remember thinking to myself that it must have been painful to chew with steel poking into their throats. Factor in that the grass looked exactly the same on both sides of the fence, and you have yourself the living definition of a dumb move. Why is it that the grass seems to always be greener on the other side of the fence? Interestingly enough, the millennial generation that I am a part of, seems to be obsessed with the notion that life is better "out there" than it is "in here." The "where" of the *out there* concept can really be best understood as *anywhere but here*. But with Jesus as the Lord of our life, this doesn't have to be the case. Our God offers us a feast, on our side of the fence, when we acknowledge His presence in the everyday. And when we stick our heads through the barbed wire, we risk doing damage to, not only our bodies, but our souls.

DISNEY WORLD

I believe contentment could be the scarcest emotion in our world today. Social media has fueled the fire of comparison and robbed many of their joy. Our desire to have, experience, and feel things outside of our current reality leads us to spend and consume in ways that we later regret.

I recently flew to Orlando, Florida with part of the staff from the church I pastor, for a conference geared at resourcing church leadership to be more effective in their local contexts. After the final morning of the conference, we were debating on what we should do, in order to make the most of our time during the beautiful weather. We discussed going to Universal Studios, Sea World, and even considered taking a fan boat ride to see the alligators in their natural habitat. After sorting through the promotional cards and making phone calls for hours and pricing, we decided to take a walk through the nature reserve, where we were staying, and lay by the pool until sunset. As we sat by the pool that evening, we discussed how good Jesus had been to us and how thankful that we were to be a part of what He was doing in the world. About that time, we noticed a plane making a straight line of white in the sky. It caught our attention. The pilot shut off whatever it was that was making the line in the sky, banked hard, and then began leaving his white trail again. We watched for ten minutes as the words "LOVE U JESUS" appeared, in all caps, immediately overhead. The words were so large and so clear that we literally began to applaud as the sky artist put the final touches on his masterpiece. It was as if God, Himself, had given us His approval on the contentment that we had experienced at the close of our trip.

Jesus' final word on the cross where He was crucified was "Tetelestai." This word was an accounting term that was spoken when the debt that was owed by someone had been paid in full. The word can be translated into English as "It is finished." Jesus was telling those in attendance, on that day, and those reading this paragraph some 2,000 years later, that the debt that was owed had been paid in full.

The book of Romans in the New Testament of the Bible tells us that we have all fallen short of the perfect standard of God's law (Chapter 3, verse 23). Even on our best day, we fail to live up to perfection. I sin constantly. Scripture also tells us that the wages of sin is death (Rom 6:23). Simply put, there is a price to be paid for the wrongdoing in my life. John 3:16 tells us that God loved us so much that He gave us Jesus. And whoever believes in the name of Jesus can be saved from the penalty of their sins. How can this be? Because He who knew no sin (Jesus, who lived a perfect life) became sin so that we might experience the forgiveness and righteousness of a perfect and holy God (2 Cor 5:21). Jesus said "it is finished" and in that moment, He defeated the curse of sin and liberated all who would believe in Him from the penalty of their faults, for all time. This, my friends, is the ultimate Good News.

Embarking on a DiscipleTrip does not grant you access to the Father. Jesus is our access and the DiscipleTrip is a product of a life that has been transformed by His goodness. You were made to be loved by the Father. You were made to enjoy His presence. You were made to extend this good news to others. And when you engage in the ancient practice of disciple-making, that began with the Son of God Himself, you are embarking on an adventure to change the world.

END OF THE DEBRIEF

At the close of our DiscipleTrip, let me encourage you to *take inventory* of what God has done, and is doing, in your heart and life. Trip Mate, you don't have to go far to see it. Look here, and not out there.

Discipleship is the cause; the church is the effect.

Live the adventure.

About the Author, Joey Cook

Joey pastors *City Church*—an urban church in Conway, Arkansas that is truly welcoming of all people, sees creativity as the key to the future, chooses authenticity over performance, substance over hype, and quality over quantity. Joey is passionate about making disciple-makers and has helped to plant five churches in the last five years.

He has a business undergrad from Arkansas State University, Masters in Theological Studies and Divinity from Liberty University Theological Seminary, and a Doctor of Ministry degree from Central Arkansas Baptist. Joey is fascinated with and committed to guiding others toward personal transformation in Jesus, fostering imagination, creating cultural change, social justice and helping others to find joy in the mundane. He, and his wife, Syndal, have 2 children; Ryder X and MJ.

Joey loves weekly date nights with Syndal, walking Banjo, the dog, around the block with his children, watching movies with the family and going on mini-adventures on the trail near their home, in Conway with the whole family.

You can email Joey at joey@citychurch.tv or connect with him online:

www.citychurch.tv  @joeycookx  @joeybcook

About the Editor, Joanna Sanders

Joanna Sanders is a graduate of Villanova University and Moody Theological Seminary. She's the founder and head writer of Colossians46.com, which provides biblical content support, writing, and editing. She loves helping other authors realize God's purpose through their stories and reflecting His glory back through their words. Joanna writes and edits for several Christian publications and publishers and has a heart for women's ministry. Joanna's book, *Fire Women: Sexual Purity and Submission for the Passionate Woman* is scheduled for release in October 2019.

Most importantly, she is wife to Geoff and mom to three godly-men-in-training.

Connect with Joanna at Colossians46.com.

Additional Resources

BCF Ministries (Biblical Counseling Foundation) bcfministries.org

DiscipleShift: Five Steps That Help Your Church to Make Disciples Who Make Disciples, Jim Putman, Bobby Harrington, with Robert E. Coleman. Zondervan, Grand Rapids, MI 2013.

The Master Plan of Evangelism, Robert Coleman. Revell, Grand Rapids, MI 2010

Discerning the Voice of God: How to Recognize When He Speaks, Priscilla Shirer. Moody Publishers, Chicago 2012

Reclaiming Surrendered Ground, Jim Logan. Moody Publishers Chicago, IL 1995.

The Essential Guide to Spiritual Warfare, Neil T. Andersson & Timothy M. Warner. Bethany House, Bloomington, MN 2016

To share your DiscipleTrip with us, please visit: DiscipleTrip.com.

 @discipletrip @discipletrip_